ISSUMATUQ

ISSUMATUQ
LEARNING FROM THE
TRADITIONAL HELPING WISDOM
OF THE CANADIAN INUIT

Kit Minor

Fernwood Publishing, Halifax

Editing: Douglas Beall
Cover drawing: Mauverneen Trainor
Inuktitut translation: Ooleepika Ikkidluak,
                        Interperter Corps, NWT
Design and production: Beverley Rach
Printed and bound in Canada.

A publication of Fernwood Publishing.

Fernwood Publishing
Box 9409 Station A
Halifax, Nova Scotia
B3K 5S3

First printing: April 1992
Second printing: December 1994

Canadian Cataloguing in Publication Data

Minor, N. Kathleen Mary.

Issumatuq

Includes bibliographical references.
ISBN 1-895686-05-9

1. Inuit -- Canada -- Social conditions. *
2. Cross-cultural counseling -- Methodology.
I. Title.

E99.E7M56 1992   305.897 1071   C92-098582-3

This book is dedicated to
Inutsiak Temoti, Simeonie, Susee,
Eric, Esau, Joe, Oleepeka, Joanisee,
Elizapee, Marisse, Tanya, Gli and Amy
and all the children of the Arctic

Contents

Forward

I first went to the Arctic in 1974 and I remained there for ten years. My first Arctic residence was Inuvik where I resided for two and a half years. When people ask me why I went to the Arctic and stayed so long, I can only respond that since I was a child I was thoroughly fascinated with the culture of the Inuit. It was something I wanted to do and a journey which opened up many wonderful and new ways of thinking and being with the world. I went to the Arctic as a Social Worker. During my time in the Arctic I was also a supervisor, regional superintendent and Chief of Staff Development and Training for the Department of Social Development, Government of the Northwest Territories.

This was an exciting time to be in the North. The Berger inquiry was a highlight of my time in Inuvik. The power of both the Inuit and Dene was obvious. Their demands to keep their cultures and their traditional approaches to presentations intact are an important and unique part of Canadian History.

From Inuvik I moved to Cambridge Bay on Victoria Island and worked with the people of Kitikmeot. I remained in this area for almost five years and it is still a place very dear to my heart. In Kitikmeot the vast majority of Social Workers were Inuit. They had some training, and mostly did Social Assistance in their home communities, a difficult task. The Social Workers asked for training and together we started Ekayuktit Nunalingna which is translated "helpers of the helpers". These community groups eventually took over much of Social Services, including hiring, distributing funds and providing a cultural based service. They advised and guided social workers through some difficult situations. We had many meetings and gatherings, working together for what the people wanted. It was a very exciting time to be in Kitikmeot.

From Kitikmeot I moved to Iqaluit where I became Regional Super-intendent of the Baffin Region. This is an enormous area covering thirteen settlements and hamlets reaching from Sanikiluaq in James bay to Grise Fiord on Ellesmere Island in the high Arctic. I lived in the Baffin Region for approximately four years. Again it was a very exciting time. I then went to live in Yellowknife, NWT for two years.

During my years in the Arctic I was privileged to hear many of the stories of the people. I heard of the famines, the coming of the whitemen, the terrible confusions which take place when a dominant group advances upon a subordinate group. Numerous Inuit asked me to write what I had learned and to relate my experiences. While I in no way consider myself to be an expert in Inuit matters—the Inuit are their own experts—I did consider the request an honour—and, thus, proceeded with the task. However, there were some informations shared with me which I was asked not to write about specifically, because other authors have left English speakers confused and have taken the material out of cultural context. I am hopeful that Inuit to come will author more information about this truly amazing group of women, men and children who have survived the harshest climate in the world with dignity and incredible caring relationships.

The reader must remember that, although the manuscript has been reviewed by many Inuit of various ages, in many locations, I am a white woman. I am not speaking for the Inuit; I am speaking of the incredible things I learned from the traditional helping wisdom of the Inuit. While I was initially preparing this document as a doctoral dissertation, I was requested by white southerners to explain some concepts in western thought. One challenge which I had put to me was: is the Inuit philosophy similar to existentialism? Initially, I said it was. However, rethinking and discussion with Inuit elders clearly brought me to the conclusion that it is something far beyond what can be stated in anglo-terminology. For this reason I have tried, where appropriate and possible, to include some terminology in Inuktitut throughout the text. A difficulty here is that some terms are in Netsilik dialect, whilst others are in Baffin dialect.

The text has taken many years to develop. I recall eight years ago meeting Errol Sharpe of Fernwood Publishing. We discussed the idea of developing a book from the material I had gathered. Throughout these many years, we have sent the manuscript throughout the Northwest Territories and received valuable feedback which has enhanced the content and accuracy.

I believe that each culture has something to offer other cultures. Now as I live in the "south" and experience some of the values and differences here, I often think of how much the Inuit have to offer, even in their daily lives. I will never forget the caring which they extend to others and the trust that is part of the Arctic.

From my work in the Arctic the "Culture-Specific Design" was developed. I began work on the design while living in Inuvik, and we began to use it in Kitikmeot working with committees. It was further used in the Baffin Region and at a workshop in the Keewatin. The design will guide the reader through insight into the Inuit culture and, particularly, traditional helping skills and approaches which, deeply rooted as they are in the cultural fabric of the Inuit, remain effective today.

Acknowledgements

I would like to express sincere appreciation to Geela Giroux, Mary Hunt, Okalik Curley, Hannah Kilabuk, Martha Michael of Iqaluit, N.W.T.; Joe Krimmerdjuar and Stevie Akpalialuk of Pangnirtung N.W.T.; Rhoda Kayakjuak of Arctic Bay; Elizapee Allakariallak of Resolute Bay. Appitaq Enuraq of Pond Inlet; Jayko Jaypoody of Clyde River; Leah Otak of Igloolik; Donald Havioyak of Coppermine, Quyutinuarq of Gjoa Haven; Attima Sallerina of Spence Bay, Ittimanqark, Monica, and Macabe and Delarosa Nartok of Pelly Bay; Sarah Ikpak and Johnny Cookie of Sanikaluaq. Their comments and suggestions proved most valuable in the construction of this book. Each took time to review the contents of the work, and listen to ideas and concerns of the author. The extent of their contributions must be sincerely acknowledged.

I also wish to thank Bob Cowsill and Barbara Britton of Yellowknife, N.W.T., David Hoe of Ottawa, Lauri Jones of Thunder Bay, Bonnie Dickie of Winnipeg and Moon Joyce of Toronto (all formerly of the N.W.T.), Jim Britton and Gordon Stanger formerly with the Department of Social Development in Yellowknife, who were both particularly supportive of my work. I thank Ellen Minor of Regina who has always supported my endeavours, even when they took me miles away. Thanks Ma. Allen Ivey of University of Massachusetts, Amherst, has been supportive since our first meeting several years ago in Yellowknife. He has regularly offered comments and suggestions, and expressed confidence in my work when it was most needed, as well as being a dedicated dissertation advisor. Thank you Allen. I thank the faculty of the Department of Social Work, Lakehead University: particularly, Roger Delaney, Mary Lou Keley and Linda Robinson, all of whom have encouraged me in my work, provided insight and are part of a wonderful academic working environment. In particular, I thank Dr. Connie Nelson, Director of Graduate Studies and Research and Associate Professor of Social Work, Lakehead University who has spent numerous hours reading and rereading each draft with great patience and insight. Her comments and suggestions were vital. I am very privileged to have such a fine colleague and friend. Thank you Connie. I thank Errol Sharpe of Fernwood Publishing who has supported and encouraged me in this project for several years. I also thank Douglas Beall of Halifax who's editorial expertise is invaluable. Finally Lauren McKinnon, both a dear friend and gifted colleague, has encouraged, supported and provided many insights to this work as well as many other academic pursuits. Thank you Lauren.

While I am responsible for errors and omissions in this text, each of the above and many others, too numerous to mention, have contributed greatly to this work over the many years.

I am grateful to each. Kujannamik!

Kitty Minor
Pπ
Thunder Bay, Canada
February, 1992

Introduction

The Canadian Inuit[1] have survived for centuries in an environment that outsiders have viewed as hostile to human life. Yet the Inuit have managed to survive and enhance their lifestyle, ensured the survival of future generations and provided a healthy psychological and emotional environment for themselves. These positive characteristics of Inuit culture have received relatively little attention. But, as any visitor who has stayed in the Arctic for any extended period of time will confirm, if one is to survive in this region even today, one would do best to have respect for and an ability to use some of the traditional notions and skills of the Inuit.

I would like to introduce the reader to some of the hardships and struggles of physical survival in the Arctic, to some of the skills and techniques developed by the Inuit to deal with these difficulties, and to the Inuit's traditional values of cooperation, sharing and trust. By focusing upon the Inuit's ways of insuring their physical, psychological and social survival, I wish to arrive at some understanding of the helping skills and approaches the Inuit have used effectively for generation upon generation in the Canadian Arctic. The reader will also be introduced to some of the cultural visitors and intruders who have affected Inuit culture and in some cases greatly changed it, for example, the missionaries who introduced Christianity. I will also focus upon the modern young Inuk and her or his adaptation to Inuit cultural teachings and the intrusion of white bureaucracy and power in the Arctic.

Our Method of Exploration

Of assistance in this exploration will be the "culture-specific design," which forms the basic outline of this book. This design was created as a guide for helpers, to enable them to understand some of the critical traditional helping components of another culture.

I developed this design while I was living in the Arctic, specifically to enhance cultural understandings, especially as they relate to helping; but in using the design, I found vast realms of information useful across, for example, the disciplines of medicine, psychiatry and education.

It must be remembered that the design was developed for use by those in the helping fields and in education. Though some anthropological tools are utilized, this book does not attempt to cover anthropological cross-cultural views in depth. The main focus is upon the traditional concepts of Inuit culture that promoted group harmony and individual self-satisfaction.

The design is composed of three levels (with Level II being subdivided into two parts): Level I is the physical survival of the group and Level IIA is the psychological and social survival of the group. Level IIB includes external influences upon the culture such as cultural visitors and unwelcomed intruders. The most critical aspects of Level IIB will be discussed as they relate to traditional helping approaches. Those not discussed will be included in a later text. Level III of the design is the adaptation of the individual cultural member to the group.

It is critical to understand that the levels are interwoven and dependent upon every aspect of the design. Further, the design is in constant flow, with each variable affecting other variables. It should be viewed as three-dimensional. Though each level has separate categories, the reader must realize that these are not definite and distinct but influence the other levels. For example, shamanism is included under physical survival, but it has definite influences at all levels. Table 1 provides an outline of the culture-specific design. Each of the following chapters will focus upon each of these levels with respect to Inuit culture.

The culture-specific design will be discussed below and is also formally summarized in Appendix 1. Appendix 2 provides a guide to the translations of key Inuit concepts from Inuktitut.

A Design for Culture-Specific Helping

The culture-specific design provides an opportunity to incorporate cultural participation and identify traditional techniques and healers within a culture. My experiences are for the most part working within singular cultures, for example, the Canadian Inuit, and specifically several different Inuit groups; Dogrib; Northern Cree; and Ojibwa. I want to share some of the knowledge I gained through these experiences and a design that was developed with Inuit of Kitikmeot and later improved upon by the involvement of Inuit from Keewatin and the Baffin region. This

Table 1 Summary of the Culture-Specific Design

Level I: Physical Survival of the Group

Inuk and nature Environmental influences Spiritual beliefs and Shamanism The concept of the souls Rituals and taboos Philosophy	These terms are defined by the group and reveal its self-understanding, each term is understood as it relates to the others, and the culture's understanding of them is a direct outcome of the survival problem.

Level IIA: Psychological and Social Survival of the Group

Family group
  kinship
  social organization
  authority
Behaviour
  customs
  rules
  ethics and morals
  values
Mind
  thought patterns
  concepts of the whole
    opposites and time
Language
  spoken language
  non-verbal communication
Transmission of the culture
  oral tradition
  art
  music
  dance
  storytelling
	These culture-specific areas are defined in a consequential relationship to Level I. They are realistic to the group and so the group's world view comes into focus.

Level IIB: External Influences upon the Culture

Intercultural influences	These come from outside the culture and may cause change within the group and the individual.

Level III: The Individual

Value to the group Safety and fulfillment of needs Acceptance by the group Identity Individuality	The individual is understood by himself and others according to the context in which he or she lives, as defined at Levels I and II. Thus individuals make sense of the world around them.

design has proven successful with four other general groups of Inuit and eight groups of Canadian Indians. The total number of participants was well over two hundred. The result of these gatherings was increased cultural awareness specific to their group, increased respect for and knowledge of traditional healing skills, and a desire by participants to learn and employ these culturally inherited skills. The design is a simple method of categorizing information and viewing some of the factors that affect the group, the individual and the environment.

A culture-specific helping approach begins with the exploration of the traditional helping systems within a group. Such an exploration is accomplished with the aid of anthropological information, which pro-vides some guidelines. The effectiveness of traditional approaches is not to be underestimated, any more than one can ignore the strength of traditional ties in helping patterns (Nobels 1972, 1974). Studies reveal that specific psychological traits and value systems are particular to cultural groups and that, in the role of helping, a helper must not only be aware of the differences but must accommodate clients by offering approaches which fit their world views. The many studies of American minority groups lend undeniable support to the concept of culturally specific approaches. The argument is strong: removal from one's geographical and cultural home and the almost inevitable generational displacement that has accompanied this removal have not managed to destroy the traditional philosophy, psychology and values basic to the culture (Delaney 1972; Jackson 1976, 1980; Jones 1980; Kitano and Sue 1973; Nobels 1972, 1974; Sue 1977). Helping needs to be developed or adapted with approaches peculiar to the history and current needs of the culture. This is a basic premise of culture-specific helping.

In contrast, cross-cultural helping stresses the development of train-ing programs to prepare helpers who will work with groups with another single culture or multicultures. The trainee gathers information and feedback from members of the cultural group and strives to win support, trust and ultimately acceptance from its members. The would-be helpers thus find themselves in a collaborative relationship. The design of these projects centres upon what the helper can learn of the culture, rather than upon the culture's definitions and decisions about what are appropriate helping skills. Although the intention of cross-cultural helping is to focus upon significant variables that are consistent with the values of the group and critical to its healthy self-image and well-being as it defines these things, the feasibility of attaining this goal is questionable. The difficulties inherent in such a project are (1) locating and defining these variables, (2) investigating the traditional approaches to psychological healing and determining how they achieve validity, (3) meshing the appropriate design of therapist/group relations with ongoing cultural changes within the group itself, and (4) since the concept of a cross-cultural helper implies that the helper is from another culture, locating and employing traditional approaches that the group found appropriate in the past.

An Investigative Design

This design was developed for use in culture-specific social work, with major emphasis upon helping. I developed it while working with the Canadian Inuit between 1974 and 1984. The design is particular to the Inuit, for example, in the separation of physical from social and psychological survival, and in the use of specific Inuit terminology at Level I. However, the design has also been used with many Canadian Indian and Métis groups, and with several other cultures. For example, it was the basis for the development of culturally specific counseling with the Igbo culture of Africa (Nwachuku and Ivey 1989). When using the design with other cultures, modifications may be needed so as not to impose another group's variables and values on that culture.

Training in a cross-cultural setting employs a member of the culture to assist in bringing the therapist to a greater degree of cross-cultural awareness, knowledge and skills (Ivey 1977, 1980; Pedersen 1976, 1977). This direct cultural coaching is necessary for a well-informed relationship. However, there is something backward about this approach. The helper has already received training— most likely in a Western institution—and, having demonstrated that she or he has acquired helping skills, now embarks upon a career in another culture. What is assumed is that cultural awareness is secondary to training as a helper. Although this assumption is seldom explicit, it persists as a dominant theme in much of the current literature.

The need for helpers is universal, from the South Pacific islands to the Canadian Arctic. But also universal is the need to tailor the methods of the helping process to the highly specific cultural situation of the client. It is more effective to encourage individuals to develop approaches to helping within their familiar cultural setting than it is to expect clients to adjust to some universal criteria or techniques of helping. Though it cannot be assumed that all indigenous persons automatically possess cultural expertise (Ivey 1980, 1981; Jackson 1980), it is realistic to hold that the majority of members of a given culture will have greater awareness, tolerance and understanding of even the most simple cultural patterns than will a non-member.

Following the recent literature, the basic problem has been redefined: We must place primary concern upon facilitating and encouraging skills and approaches that will be effective in the arena where they will be applied. Rather than employing helpers from outside the culture, the emphasis should now shift to a search for helpers located within the group—individuals who have already been acknowledged by their cultural group to possess particular helping skills. A helper from outside the culture can be a facilitator, an investigator and a source of support, but should not be a director or an imposer of foreign theories. Ivey (1980, 42) states:

> Choosing an appropriate theory and method demands that the helper make decisions based on personal, cultural, language and/or social differences. The process and goals of helping should match the personal and cultural background of the client.

This can be effectively achieved by an indigenous helper within the specific cultural setting.

I do not intend to presume that this design works in cross-cultural or multicultural settings. Commonalities of all the groups who have participated in the culture-specific design in Canada are a similar set of political issues and extraneous influences upon their groups. Other groups may have other realities to attend to that may require modification of the design, and indeed in some cases the design may not be applicable for culture-specific helping.

Those who wish to assist in the development of effective helping designs need to centre upon the specific characteristics of the culture at hand and allow its indigenous members to define the most appropriate approach to helping. Ideally, all those involved would be members of the specific culture, including the facilitator. If outside helpers are to be involved, they must recognize and accept the limits of their potential knowledge and expertise and help to foster unique, creative styles of helping that are appropriate to the environment and specific to the individual needs of the client group by whom the service is required and requested—thus, a culture-specific model.

Applications of this model are intended to be made in specific cultural settings. These are not to be confused with general intercultural or multicultural settings for which different approaches and alternative techniques would be called for, although some aspects of the design and methodology may be applicable and borrowed.

Steps in Creating a Culture-Specific Design

To ensure that the design of a culture-specific helping program is rooted in the culture and appropriate to it, as well as politically and administratively viable, three steps are necessary:

1. to ensure the participation and leadership of knowledgeable, articulate and influential members of the culture,
2. to explore, identify and understand the philosophy, psychology and traditional patterns of interpersonal interaction that prevail within the group, and
3. to embark upon a program of helping that involves support and facilitation and has evaluative criteria built into the design to monitor the effectiveness of the efforts, so truly culture-specific helping may be provided.

Responsibility must become a two-way process, something like a transaction, in which concern for others is exchanged for an understanding of each other and what is appropriate in the helping context. If a non-member is to have a role in the process of helping, that role should be as a supportive facilitator. The members of the specific culture should become the initiators, leaders, designers and ultimately the ones who will take responsibility for application, ongoing re-evaluation and initiation of change. The design can be used within cultures to clarify traditional and changing lifestyles. The method is to dialogue at each level and the sub-levels within. This is a long process, in which facilitating skills, dialogue and participation by members are critical components.

Step 1: Control and Direction from Within
The fact is that native members of a specific culture are the most reliable experts in the techniques of emotional, psychological and physical survival within the bounds of that culture and its environment. An example of this has been the capacity of the Inuit to survive in an environment where others perished physically, emotionally and psychologically. In the Arctic, others became dependent upon and embraced the Inuit world view in order to survive. The choice was simple: either accept and adapt to the Inuit philosophy or die. Even today, with various modern technologies and changes in the Arctic, cultural visitors continue to need to gain a respect for the environment, adapt to certain foods and learn some traditional survival techniques.

This example may appear extreme to some because of the severity of the climate and the psychological factors in the Arctic, but the fundamental relationships are parallel whenever one studies other cultures. Culture enables people to survive in a given natural environment, and those who are born into that culture understand it best. Unfortunately, in most cultures the need for adjustments and adaptations is more subtle and hence more easily hidden from non-members who assume that the knowledge embedded in such cultures is unnecessary to their own survival. South Africa is one example. In all too many such cases, outsiders have succeeded in maintaining their own world views and have even been able to impose these views on the environment and make changes to the cultural fabric of the indigenous people (Brody 1975, 1976; Delany 1972; Fanon 1968; Mead 1955, 1978).

Thus far, the emphasis has been upon control and power from within a culture. This must be realized in the context of adaptation to the bureaucratic demands and technological advantages of a white-dominated world. Negation of this axiom could prove to be to the greater disadvantage of a people. My experiences in emphasizing indigenous helping techniques among the Canada Inuit brought to light the necessity of heeding and adapting to outside influences such as the Northwest Territories and Canadian governments. However, Step 1 of the design still applies: cultural members must control and contribute to the process.

Step 2: Defining "Culture-Specific"

> Sometimes we tend to confuse race and ethnic groups with culture. Great races do have different cultures. Ethnic groups within races differ in cultural content. But, people of the same racial origin and of the same ethnic groups differ in their cultural matrices. All browns, or blacks or others, or yellows, or reds are not alike in the cultures in which they live and have their being. The understanding of another, or of groups other than our own, demands a knowledge of varied elements within a culture as the variety of culture components within a larger cultural matrix (Moore 1974, 41).

It is important to determine the "varied elements" that distinguish culture and ethnicity and thus the helping system that is most sensible in application. Jackson (1976, 1980) and Nobels (1972, 1974) focus upon the commonalities of family structure and group identification among African and American Blacks. Jackson (1980) uses the concept of "continual flexibility in circularity" that was first introduced by Brown (cited ibid.). This notion located traditional helping approaches within the originating culture, but provides for their flexible application and finally describes their evolution and maintenance as a kind of circular inter-responsibility that holds between helping and survival.

How does one systematically investigate the helping processes of a culture, whether one is of that culture or another? To shed light on this, I have worked on developing a phase approach, based upon field work and academic research.

I started with the assumption that physical survival is the basic entry-level notion, that this notion will provide entry into the patterns of interaction that take place within the group at the level of survival. Thus, investigations of culture-specific helping begin at Level I, the physical survival of the group. Study of Level I will assist in the identification of factors in traditional group helping that have been essential to group survival. This level provides guidelines for identifying the effects of the natural environment upon the group. The names assigned to each area are English and are as close to the translation from Inuktitut as possible (see Figure 1 for the terms used at each level).Obviously, in working with a group with a language other than English, the terms need translation and/or modification. This in itself caused much discussion and debate, and resulted in some modifications by Inuit participants to show what was important at each level and what was the most accurate terminology in Inuktitut. This procedure resulted in more Inuit ownership of the process.

Investigation at Level IIA of the design will reveal factors in the world view of the group critical to social and psychological survival. This information will make sense if it is understood to have a dependent relationship on the discoveries made at Level I. The critical aspect of exploration through this design is that the investigator must not strive to understand the system from the perspective of a world view other than that of the group under study. This system should assist Inuit and members of non-Western or minority cultures to explore their own culture "from within," gain some understanding of the origins of their own world views and identify approaches to living and helping that were previously taken for granted and hence unnoticed.

Level IIB investigates the extraneous influences that affect a culture. These influences come from outside the culture, and their effects can be realized once physical and psychological survival are understood. External influences include other cultures' politics, media, technologies, religions and educational systems.

Level III provides an opportunity to make sense of the individual within the group and shows what is gained when the individual is valued as a member, and what is lost when the person ceases to be valued. This understanding is achieved through dialogue, song, rituals, and other cultural expressions.

Once the inquirer reaches Level III patterns of behaviour, the culture's thought and traditional helping techniques will emerge and make sense as a group function. It is critical at this level to identify these phenomena within the individual. Application of Ivey and Gluckstern's (1976) design of micro-helping has proved effective in identifying culture- specifics

Figure 1. Inuktitut Terminology Employed in the Culture-Specific Design

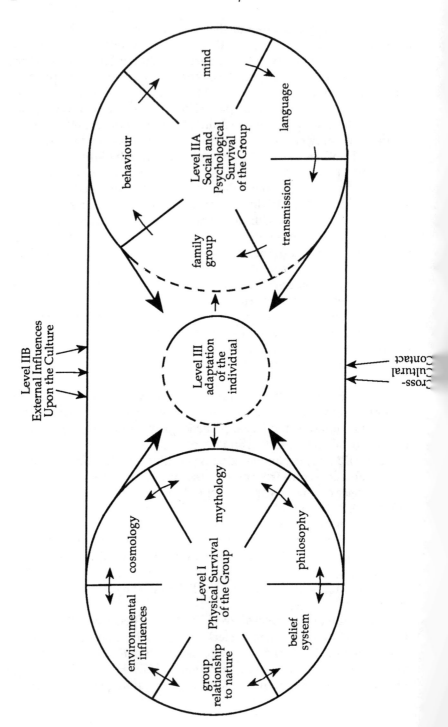

and the meaning of behaviours within a group. I have used this method with success to facilitate the development of culture-specific helping among the Canadian Inuit. It was critical that members of the cultural group participate in these activities and share responsibility for interpreting behaviour.

Empathic understanding, respect and authenticity (Rogers 1942, 1957, 1970) are necessary in all helping roles. Helpers establish themselves as caring people through establishing their interest in helping. However, the methods, approaches and practices used need to be specific to the context and should be based upon the group or individual's experience. To demonstrate empathy, congruence and positive regard, the helper must accept, respect and apply culturally appropriate means and possess the awareness, knowledge and skills necessary to effect competent communication within that context. The appropriate and logical approach demands utilization of membership participation and acknowledgement of the helpers present within the group, and the incorporation of much of the traditional helping approach of that specific culture. The cultural visitor may become a facilitator if requested to be so by the group.

The design begins with environmental factors, moves on to psychological and sociological factors and then moves to a realistic, clear and consistent view of the individual. The drawbacks of the design also serve as its checkpoints, because the design cannot be carried out without the full cooperation of group members, and attempts to apply the design will fail if one attempts to impose views and values upon the group members with whom one is working. For example, silence is a traditional helping skill among the Inuit and is respected. The facilitator who speaks too much will be ignored. Chapters 1 to 4 will explore other traditional skills and approaches of the Inuit. As the design is constructed, the process of gaining cultural experience itself is lengthy and as complicated as the helping process, and neither can be achieved in a short time.

Step 3: Support, Facilitation and Testing

Culture-specific helping requires that the investigator facilitate and support the process, and possess the skills necessary to identify culturally relevant patterns and behaviours. The investigator must be able to dialogue, use questions within the framework of the culture and glean important information, analyses, etc. This individual should possess the investigative awareness and curiosity of an anthropologist.

Continual testing of the appropriateness of the design and close evaluation of its benefits to clients are essential to its continued effectiveness. Further, flexibility within the design, dependent upon the culture, is important. Testing itself is a difficult matter, involving culture-specific approaches and sensitivity, and requires further attention and study. The usual statistical studies, questionnaires and other baggage of academic psychologists may be starkly out of concert with the folkways of small and tribally organized cultures or camps. For example, while facilitating a culture-specific workshop in the Keewatin, I suggested an evaluation. A written evaluation was determined to be not appropriate, so several alternatives were discussed and it was decided that a metaphorical evaluation would be appropriate. Thus, each participant told a story about her or his experiences over the preceding three days. In general, approaches to testing and evaluation must be developed within the context of the culture at hand, but it should be obvious that further experimentation and refinement of techniques remain to be accomplished.

Using the Culture-Specific Design

This design is not for anthropological research but rather is a tool to assist helpers and social workers to provide more effective and culturally appropriate helping within a specific culture. The implementation of the design is for the purpose and teaching of helping with cultural appropriateness, and thus the focus of the design is upon those areas most pertinent to helping.

The reader should note four things. First, the design is meant to guide the reader in pursuit of information. In this book, the areas of exploration are some of the approaches to helping that were traditionally employed by the Inuit. Thus every effort is made to investigate the aspects of the design that have had the greatest effect upon helping. Effort is made to provide the reader with an insight into the influences of nature, belief systems, philosophy, psychology, relationships, external factors and the modern Inuk, and the importance of traditional concepts and some effects these concepts have today. However, it must also be noted that I am a white Westerner and this will influence the investigation. To provide the reader with succinct and factual information, the assistance of several Inuit colleagues was sought, and their guidance proved very helpful.

Second, though the design uses terms as outlined, in order to have the material make sense in the Inuit world view, it was necessary to have the section headings reflect terms common to the Inuit. To do otherwise would be to impose a world view other than that of the Inuit culture. The world view of the Inuit was also used in the discussion of family groups. The importance and complexity of Inuit relationships to necessitate this. Readers who wish to apply the design to other cultures may need to adapt some terms to suit that other culture and reflect its uniqueness.

Third, though this book refers to various Inuit groups, the concepts presented may not be transferable in total to all Inuit groups. For example, though the design has been effective in the Canadian Arctic, it may be less effective in Alaska. This text reviews and sheds some light upon general characteristics of the Canadian Inuit, but it should be noted that I lived and worked with distinct groups: the Netsilingmiut, Utkuhikhalingmiut, Arvilinghuarmiut and Copper Inuit of Kitikmeot (central Arctic); the Igloolingmiut of the Igloolik area; the Sanikiluaq group of the Belcher Islands; and groups of the Baffin region. I also conducted a workshop in the Keewatin. The materials contained herein are provided to give the reader insight into the traditional ways. However, these notions do not apply specifically to every Inuk or every group, and this is clearly not intended. Just as every society contains peculiarities and differences, so does that of the Inuit.

Finally, the design is in constant motion. Each level is constantly affecting all other levels in a variety of directions. The momentum of the culture depends on each individual member's reaction to each level, and on the reaction of each and all groups within the culture. The flow of the culture can vary from equilibrium to chaos, depending upon the stability of flow at each level and the effect of each level upon the other.

The Inuit are a group separate from the Indians and the Dene. Traditionally, the Inuit have occupied areas of Canada north of the tree line and thus reside on the tundra. For the most part, it was not until the nineteenth century that any form of regular contact took place between the Inuit and other cultures. Prior to influences from other groups, the Inuit were nomadic, survived by hunting and gathering, and lived in small, well organized camp groupings (Minor and Turner 1986). These camps consisted of usually one to three extended family networks, including the nuclear families contained within each network. On occasion, and in particular areas, larger networks did camp together. The camps moved to seasonal hunting and fishing areas several times a year. Throughout this book the term *camp* will refer to this traditional living style of the Inuit. Since the intrusion of Western cultures, many changes have taken place in the Inuit lifestyle. However, strong currents of the traditional culture remain. This book will investigate that traditional system, both its strengths and weaknesses, and will also provide a glimpse of the confusions caused when a culture is in transition.

This text identifies some techniques of psychological healing developed in traditional Inuit culture to aid individuals during times of stress. The particular aspects of personal interaction under investigation are those that proved useful in reducing anxiety and freed camp members to participate in *collaborative relationships (sanaqatigiingniq)* for community survival.

The cultural characteristics of a group are acquired through historical developments. A culture is the totality of the lifestyles of a people and includes the arts, morals, knowledge, beliefs, customs, laws, capabilities and habits of its individual members. Within a culture, patterns arise that are obvious to the group. Benedict (1934) states that such characteristics have a useful function in a particular culture. Such characteristics need to be understood in the light of the emotionality, intellect, world view and functional perspective of that culture.

Within various cultures the role of the helper has often been highly significant. In cultures like that of the Canadian Inuit, the role of such individuals has been difficult for outsiders to ascertain. However, recent culturally specific investigations have revealed unique and valuable repositories of skills and customs used to help members of traditional groups (Minor 1979, 1980a, 1980b; Nelson, Kelley and McPherson 1985; O'Neil 1979).

Ruben outlines several important dimensions of intercultural competence. Basically these dimensions involve capacities to communicate respect, be nonjudgmental, be personable, display empathy, be flexible and maintain a tolerance for ambiguity. He notes that effective communication, both verbal and non-verbal, must be emphasized and that one must maintain an alertness and sensitivity to the needs, values, aspirations and ways of the other (Ruben 1977, 471-72).

In order to develop an awareness of the helping approaches employed by the "traditional Inuit"[2] in *interpersonal relationships (inuuqatigiingniq)* and their effect upon the present culture, it is necessary to have some comprehension of three areas that exerted tremendous influence on the interactions of the Inuit: environmental factors, spiritual beliefs, shamanism, and philosophy, all deemed necessary for physical survival;[3] the complex and highly structured network of human relationships; and the external influences upon the Inuit from other cultures. Elderly informants verify the presence and critical importance of these areas prior to the steady involvement of non-Inuits *(qallunaaq).*[4] Because this book deals with traditional interpersonal helping skills, I shall initially confine my comments to the earlier communal patterns and then later will note aspects of the modern community life of the Inuit.

Chapter 1

The Physical Survival of the Group

The skills and traditional concepts of the Inuit assisted the group in physical survival. Traditional Inuit philosophy and belief systems, the concept of two souls, and taboos and rituals joined together to create camp harmony.

Inuit and Nature

Just to Survive

I have walked upon this land and I have known
the sweeping cold winds of winter.
I have travelled on the oceans and the Great Bay of Hudson.
The sun has sank deep upon the horizon for many days,
and has then returned
to cast a timeless light upon the Great Mother Earth.
I have known these things for many years,
and still I gaze in wonder.
And I have known the people of the land,
they are my friends and I am theirs.
Together we have travelled and shared and sometimes
we were cold and hungry,
and it hurt, together.
There is a mystery to this land, the blending of
woman/man and nature,
to the tranquil awareness of reality,
a gentle acceptance of the past presenting the

present and molding the future.
And a gentle, firm and dramatic struggle to
survive . . . just to survive (Minor, in progress).[5]

The Inuit were constantly aware of the reality of struggle. Study of the hardships inherent in the Inuit way of life reveals that, in order to physically survive and maintain a flow of cooperation, a stable emotional balance within the camp was essential. Personal tragedies had to be overcome as quickly as possible and with a minimum of disruption to the entire camp. Overconcern with emotional problems could lead to a dangerously expensive expenditure of energy. This could affect total camp harmony and place efforts for physical survival below those for emotional balance. In the Arctic, where starvation was common, this could not be tolerated.

The hardships of the traditional Inuit way of life are clearly pointed out by Bob Barnabus, an Inuk from the Arctic Bay area:

> I started to hunt when I was sixteen. In summertime it was very enjoyable, but in the winter, when we were hungry, it was difficult and not pleasant at all. In those days before we were with the Qallunaat, the Inuit used to hunt to the best of their ability. There were periods of hunger when people died of starvation; my grandfather and my uncle died that way. Sometimes we had to eat dogs that had already starved to death and sometimes people would eat other people. On cold winter mornings, we had to put on frozen clothes when we awoke. That is how we used to be (Innukshuk and Cowan 1976, 177).

Nuligak, from the Tuktoyaktuk area, further emphasizes the harsh traditional realities:

> From time immemorial the Inuit have looked for something to eat and have gone hunting for it. How many hunters have remained in the bush for days and days and come back without a single caribou! Forty or fifty below zero at times, and sometimes colder than that, and having left home without eating they had to stay two or three days without food. There were caribou, but not a cloud in the sky— no way of getting near them. . . . I have seen men freeze their cheeks, their noses, their feet. Cold masters us quickly when the stomach is empty. A hunter is powerless in a blizzard, and when the weather is fine and clear it is impossible to get near anything! (Nuligak 1966, 133).

Father Antonin Mouchard wrote in his diary on September 30, 1943:

> The Eskimos who were on the hunting expedition returned. Starving and mere skeletons they rejoined the other miserable people of the camp who are no better off than themselves. The hunters returned with empty hands. It is a tragic situation, a struggle against death by starvation. All the bones and other rottenness have been carefully picked up in order that we could give something to our stomachs which cry famine (*Link*, May 1945).

With these examples, we face the realities of the Inuit fight for physical survival and are provided a glimpse of the background conditions of their general attitude towards emotional upset. The Inuit recognized that simple physical survival must claim priority over all other concerns. All energy had to be expended in their will to survive the elements, and skills were developed and utilized to reduce emotional discontent or trauma. In the Canadian Arctic, it would be suicide for a camp to become engrossed in emotional disharmony or to allow a productive camp member to indulge in remorseful seclusion.

> Permanent homes they had none; life was a perpetual wandering in search of food, a wandering that ended only with death. The winter's twilight had shown me their blurred forms dragging the over burdened sleds from one sealing-ground to another to escape the threat of famine; and the midnight sun shone on husband, wife and little daughter, weighted down with heavy packs, stumbling over the stackless land to a new fishing lake in the hope of breaking their fast before, and then sleep. Food, clothing and shelter, those primal necessities that generally come so easily to dwellers in more temperate climes, demanded from them ceaseless effort, until the desperate battle to preserve life seemed almost to nullify any purpose for life. Only an invicibly optimistic race, patient, hardy and good tempered could have wrestled with this environment and survived (Jenness 1928, 243-44).

Spiritual Beliefs and Shamanism

Any review of culture necessarily involves an investigation of the religious beliefs and philosophy of a group. Among the Inuit the traditional religion was shamanism, which appears to have since been greatly influenced by the Christian missionaries. To understand the influence of these missionaries upon the Canadian Inuit (discussed in depth in Chapter 3), it is essential to first have some knowledge of the traditional practice of shamanism,[6] whose most important rituals revolved around the figure of the shaman.

The shaman held a powerful and respected position in the Inuit culture. The individual who gained this position was believed to possess supernatural powers in many areas of life. These powers included the ability to heal the infirm, to change or influence nature to provide a more suitable environment for survival, and to cause a change in another's physical being so an individual need could be met by, for example, inducing pregnancy or correcting a malfunction of the limbs. Given such powers and abilities, the shaman was viewed as a gifted Inuk.

An Inuk might hold the position of shaman and then, over a period of time, apparently lose his or her powers. For example, success was based upon accepted visual proof of a change directed by the shaman. Should an induction by the shaman result in failure, she or he would blame this upon an action of a group member that angered the spirits, and this would be accepted by the group. However, as failures in different situations became more numerous, requests from the group for intervention by the shaman would decrease until the group consensus was that he or she had lost power and influence as a shaman and no further requests would be made. Having lost her or his power, the individual would return to a prior, unelevated role in the community, as a hunter-provider, homemaker, etc. Later in life, it was possible for the same individual to be thought to have regained this position of influence with the supernatural and once again assume the role of shaman.

The group gave recognition and respect to the individual who proved power in influencing the supernatural to the community's satisfaction. The status of the shamans in the Inuit community was therefore a reflection of their influence and status in the spirit world. Though the shamans were known within their own communities, and perhaps in other Inuit communities, an outsider would not recognize these individuals as shamans. Outsiders learned of shamans only through shared confidences with group members or the shamans themselves. This confidentiality became particularly prevalent with the intrusion of the missionaries, who viewed shamanism as evil.

Within an Inuit cooperative group, there could be more than one shaman, but within an extended family unit there would be only one. Shamanism was defined by neither sex nor age. On occasion the role of shaman would fall upon someone who had a physical or mental disability and thus the individual was provided with an essential role within the culture and served as a contributing member of society. In such cases, individual infirmities did not present themselves as a burden for the group, rather the deficit was overcome by the service the individual offered to the others. By no means was the shaman always or even frequently selected from among the infirm. For the most part, a healthy and strong individual would be acknowledged in the role of shaman. The critical factor was a sense of power, sanctioned by the extended family unit, that the individual experienced within himself or herself—power of thought, influence over others and/or physical strength. My research indicates that, in general, individuals possessing unique qualities— whether an infirmity, bodily strength or great intelligence —were often thought to possess supernatural powers and that these powers were comprised of forces within the individuals upon which they drew to perform rituals and display the "magic powers" of shamanism.

There were two categories of shaman, which were based upon the results of the shaman's exercise of power. Some shamans' attempts to cure individuals, encourage climatic changes or influence situations manifested negative consequences. The Inuit regarded this ability to make a situation worse as a sign of individual power. Fear of negative results would cause the group to avoid the power of that particular shaman. The powerful influence and authority of the shaman were recognized but were not generally sought out. However, such a shaman usually continued to use their powers with the result that they became a convenient object of blame for mishaps befalling the group.

The second type of shaman was one who was viewed as successful and usually produced positive change. These powers and the individual who embodied them were actively sought out. However, even when seeking the positive powers of a shaman, a fear of mystery and the supernatural persisted among the seekers. Yet, simultaneously, there was also a feeling of excitement and challenge, of mysticism and of the powers behind nature. Though these two categories of shaman may seem simplistic to others, recognition of them provided further harmony within the group.

Various techniques were used by the shaman to induce a requested change or determine the cause of a hardship. For example, songs and dances would be performed to induce a pregnancy in a woman who had been barren and wanted a child. In searching out a cause, such as that for poor luck in securing food, the most common ritual was that of *kilarug* (a holding down of the head). In this ceremony the shaman was assisted by another person. While the assistant lay in a prone position, a string was tied about his or her head. The shaman would hold the end of the string and, while pulling on it in a jerking motion, announce the general kind of cause being sought while simultaneously invoking the spirits to assist in determining the precise nature of the influence. Once the cause had been correctly identified, the force of the spirits upon the head of the assistant would make it impossible for the shaman to lift the string any longer. A shaman would often assign a penance to disturbed persons if the cause of their disturbance involved the breaking of a taboo. In some cases the matter would seem to remedy itself when the cause became part of conscious knowledge. My research has revealed many cases in which individuals were greatly assisted in overcoming a particular situation or disability through the powers and spiritual assistance of a shaman.

The powers of the shaman should not be underestimated. "The notion that indigenous healers are "quacks" and "frauds" and that only Western (Modern) approaches to mental health care are valid is the greater inaccuracy" (Marsella 1979). Unfortunately, historical documentation of effective cures induced by shamans among Canadian Inuit is lacking. However, there has been sufficient awareness of the shamans' power on the part of outsiders to prompt considerable thought. Reference is given to my own experiences and those documented by Boas (1888), Jenness (1928) and Rasmussen (1931). The fact that the Inuit survived as a thriving culture for more than one thousand years is in itself proof of the shamans' ability to help.

The helping role of the shaman was to ascertain the cause of personal ill-fortune, which could affect not only the individual but also bring misfortune to the whole group. The Inuit believed that non-harmonious spirits caused disturbances that upset the balance of the soul. A release of these spirits from the inflicted soul would result in harmonious well-being. Various approaches were used to discover the evil spirits, and once the source of causation was determined, the shaman prescribed a way to rid the soul of these spirits. It was generally expected that the results would be a return of the soul to its normal, natural balance and a restoration of emotional and psychological harmony among the group. This restoration of harmony would in turn allow the energies of the group to be centred upon the processes of physical survival.

The skills of the shaman were critical in recognizing when an individual or individuals had caused displeasure among the spirits and thus affected the survival of the group. The shaman knew how to appease the spirits and could thus effectively solve the matter that was causing concern to the camp members. The Inuit simply could not waste time in despair or yearning, for each day they were faced with the reality of searching for food and finding shelter. The skills of the shaman in reducing anxiety and knowing how to gain the blessings of the spirits were critical to camp well-being. Given the frequency of successful treatment by shamans, it is not surprising that the Inuit had tremendous trust in the ability of these women and men. The shaman was the healer who understood the spirits and had the power to determine methods of pleasing the spirits. This created a sense of security among the people.

> The natives trusted in their medicine-men [sic] and the medicine-men, with rare exceptions, believed themselves gifted with supernatural powers. The spirits that wander unseen came at their bidding and obeyed their commands. At times they came unsummoned, and a man [sic] raved on the hillsides or on the frozen sea where no one beheld his frenzy (Jenness 1928, 52).

The powers of the shaman were believed to balance an Inuk with nature through their effects upon the souls of individuals. To fully understand this concept, a discussion of the souls is necessary.

The Concept of Two Souls

The Inuit traditionally believed that each individual possessed two souls (*turnqaniq*)[7] —a human soul and a name soul. The *human soul* constituted the main physical strength of the individual. It gave energy, power and endurance (Balikci 1970; Minor 1979). Basically, the human soul was the visible and/or impressionable strength, skills and knowledge essential for physical survival. This soul was exterior — it could be seen, heard and acknowledged. The human soul experienced one life on earth and, following death, journeyed to an afterworld to reside in peace and harmony among the spirits. This soul was unique to each person and accounted for the individuality of the Inuk.

The *name soul* floated freely about the cosmos and possessed strengths of mind and character. The name soul was not only within the body of the Inuk but also invisibly about him or her. It could partially be characterized as personality or intellectual and emotional ability, but name souls were also infinite and shared in the cosmos. For example, a child named Kudluk was expected to have the common characteristics of all others named Kudluk. Following death, the name soul of an individual would float about until it was called upon at a naming ritual to enter a new child or, in some cases, an animal. Name souls were also viewed as guardians. Thus a child might receive several names and be considered highly endowed. Sometimes a child was named for an individual while that individual was still living. In this case, the strengths of a child's character would be decided by the individual for whom he or she was named and the soul would be shared. The strengths varied with the specific name soul, but the general characteristics remained the same for each name. If the individual for whom the child was named was dead, the inner character strengths of the child were expected to be the same as those of the deceased individual. In a sense, this concept of free-floating souls gives evidence to support an Inuit theory of reincarnation.

The traditional Inuit beliefs concerning the two souls also provide a theoretical justification for the cultural and individual acceptance of suicide, infanticide, homicide and senilicide, just as the rigourous harshness of Arctic survival in itself supports a theory of survival of the fittest. Given these factors, it would be reasonable for elderly, inform or depressed individuals to view death as a health escape, for they were guaranteed to return later through the naming ritual when things were better.

The souls were essential to Inuit philosophy and psychology, encouraging exploration for strengths of character within the name soul, while the human soul sought knowledge and the skills to survive. The souls thus combined in spiritual search and struggle.

The shamanistic influence and the concept of the souls resulted in the rituals and taboos the Inuit employed in their efforts towards physical and emotional survival. The Netsilik and Igloolik Inuit, and Inuit groups in general, emphasize the relationship between nature and the individual through traditional rituals. These beliefs have been instrumental in fostering increased psychological security in Inuit society. For the Inuit, supernatural and mythological beliefs provided explanations for all situations and, in Western terms, gave meaning to existence.

Inuit beliefs in the supernatural were particularly evident with regard to spirits and the *turnqaniq*. Within this framework, the shamans acted as mediators between the individual and the spirit world. Other crucial elements of Inuit cosmology included *tupilaks* (something feared), *tunerlaks* (spirits) dwarfs and, from the world of nature, *nuliajuk* (sea), *narsuk* (weather), *tatgag* (moon) and others (Kappi 1977; Kalluak 1974).

Rituals and Taboos

The strength and personality of an individual were gathered from the two souls and influenced by the spirits. The human soul was identified with the physical strengths and appearance of the individual. Thus the human soul was exterior and visible, and the name soul was interior and private. Further, the souls of the *natsiq* (seal), *nanuk* (bear) and *tuktu* (caribou) were revered with much ritual and circumscribed by taboo. Fear of an animal could prevail when a taboo was disregarded (Balikci 1970). The Inuit belief that animals had souls, not only as archetypes but as individuals, is similar to that concerning the name soul. Both the name soul and the animal soul were "free floating," i.e., continuous and eternal in the cosmos. Upon the death of an animal, if taboos were properly observed by the hunter, it was believed that the animal's soul would re-enter a new animal for the same hunter to pursue again. Should taboos be ignored, this soul remained free-floating in the cosmos without influence upon the people; these animal souls would not join a new animal and thus there would be no game to hunt.

Amulets were carried by both men and women, particularly those of the Netsilik and Igloolik groups. Usually children were given amulets when young and these were carried through life, for amulets were thought to retain their power throughout the lifetime of the carrier. The amulets conferred protection and acted as a medium between the bearer and the supernatural. Amulets were considered an aid in the daily course of survival and were elements in the complex of activities the Inuit knew as helping (Rasmussen 1931; Balikci 1970).

Each Inuk was believed to possess a group of his or her own spirits, and the potential evil these spirits could effect was a constant theme of individual awareness. Individual means to ensure positive assistance from the spirits lay in maintaining deep respect for and strict observance of rituals and taboos. To the Inuit, the struggle to survive was a harsh reality, a tremendous test of endurance that would be fruitless and futile without the cooperation and assistance of the spirits. The strong, persistent and fearless individual was given the highest respect, because it was considered that such a person used the most positive influences of the spirits and would be highly rewarded in the afterlife.

The religious practices of the Netsilingmiut[8] can be divided into two general areas which were considerably hedged by taboos. One area of taboos involved the hunt. Rasmussen (1931) emphasizes the taboos surrounding hunting activity, such as prohibition of hunting at particular times. The second general area of taboos centred around the human individual. For example, strict ritual was to be observed with respect to childbirth and menstruation. In childbirth, depending on the group, the husband was allowed or not allowed to assist. The woman always delivered the child in a kneeling position and the infant was either wiped or licked clean. Following the birth, the child and the mother resided in isolation for a full moon cycle and during this time the mother did not indulge in intercourse. She could only eat food provided to her by her husband. Some bands had more taboos and rituals than others, and these practices varied from group to group.

Taboos provided symbolic significance to important activities and gave the individual and the community a sense of security and well-being in a harsh, unpredictable environment. Proper observation of taboos psychologically guaranteed success, and hardships were often explained as resulting from a breach of taboo.

The observance of rituals and taboos depended upon the individuals, but their results, positive or negative, affected the entire group. Communalism was integrated with the supernatural, because the spiritual consequences of each individual's activities had immediate affects upon everyone. While religious beliefs, including rituals, taboos and shamanism, satisfied the inquiries of the mind about the whys and wherefores of a rigourous life, they also provided the core tools of stable mental health or, at least, defense against psychological distress in a harsh environment. The powers of the shaman and the rituals and taboos observed by the early Inuit constituted a particularly effective spiritual world. These religious beliefs were suited to the general culture and provided meaning to and comprehension of life's struggles and joys. Thus they had definite bearing upon helping or affecting the group psychology. These cultural values allowed a strong and adaptable social group to flourish within their physical surroundings.

Traditional Philosophy

The traditional philosophy of the Inuit attended to three principles in the search towards meaning in life: (1) acting to assist the group, (2) experiencing group values such as love and nature and (3) suffering together. The struggles of the Inuit just to survive provided a constant journey. During the interviews I conducted, a tremendous emphasis upon the individual will to explore was repeatedly encountered. Setting new goals for oneself and responding to new challenges for the benefit of the group was highly valued. Here is an example of individual self-exploration with the ultimate goal being the benefit of the group:

> My early years were a challenge. It was always a learning experience. At times my life was hard, but it was also a life full of new goals and accomplishments. It was a life full of cooperation among camp members, deep spiritual satisfaction and inner contentment (Etoagant Akohayook, personal interview, Pangnirtung, October 3, 1979).

Older informants stated that their lives were a constant spiritual preparation and that the challenges of life were those of the mind as well as those of physical endurance, both focused on group survival. This concept is different from the Western emphasis on individual accomplishments and goals; rather the focus was upon each person developing strengths and abilities that enhanced the group. Each took on roles and activities in a group effort. If each pulled their weight, the group benefitted.

This way of the Inuit is in accord with the view which holds that "the goal of therapy is not to strengthen the client's ego, but to encourage the client to transcend the ego by experiencing the self as embedded in and expressive of the community. . . . Symptoms are transformed into elements of social categories rather than personal states" (Lafromboise 1988, 392).

I asked an elderly Inuk what was important to her in life. She gazed at me for a long time and began to speak in Inuktitut. As we looked out over Hudson's Bay towards a distant peninsula, she said, "Do you see that hill over there? I replied yes. She continued, "Do you see the hill beyond that? I again said yes. She then paused and with a smile asked, "And do you see the hill beyond that? I looked at her and said no. She smiled and said, "Yes, but we know it is there and if we join together we will find it, together." We then talked for many hours of the many struggles that her camp had endured during her life, and throughout the conversation she continually referred to the group effort, with no reference to individual accomplishment (Sarah, personal interview, Sanikiluaq, 1980).

Unlike the Europeans, the Inuit did not indulge in great material preparations. Though the Inuit did cache food for long winter months, they did not hoard it. Rather, they stored an amount sufficient to provide for themselves through hard times. Beyond that, the Inuit had a constant dependence and reliance upon nature. It is crucial to understand that the essence of the Inuit group effort was comprised of spiritual exploration and not material preparation.

Spiritual preparation began at a very early age and was greatly influenced by an individual's parents and grandparents. The elderly I have interviewed often referred to the love and respect they held for their parents. Their homes, whether caribou tent or igloo, were filled with companionship and caring. It was a sparse home which contained only what was essential for physical survival, but it was also full of whatever was necessary for its occupants' inner spiritual needs. As the young Inuk grew to early adulthood, he or she learned the meaning of struggle and many times suffered and learned to endure hardships. Confronting these difficulties created a realization of one's own importance, strengths and weaknesses. As a youth, the Inuk gradually came to appreciate the necessity for group interaction and deep, quiet caring of others. One's world and life had a meaning: to grow constantly, to learn, to develop one's inner being, and to teach others the lessons for the survival of the people.

Having reviewed the work of some of those who participated in the movement of Existential Psychology (Frankl 1967, 1970; Maslow 1968, 1976; May 1969; Allport 1978) and having held many interviews with

Inuit with regard to the concepts of their traditional psychology, I conclude that an Existential approach can help in understanding the Inuit tradition. For the sake of explanation and understanding, the phenomena of suicide will be particularly investigated.

Suicide was most common among the elderly and was considered a reasonable approach to death for them. The concept was clear: individuals spent a lifetime in spiritual preparation and struggle and, as they approached old age and became a burden upon the group, they would realize that there was only one way to alleviate the burden, and that was by death. This decision was arrived at through the process of *ajurnarmat*[9] a logical approach to problem-solving, where a matter was clearly considered and a decision was made as to whether or not something could be done about it. If nothing could be done, it was accepted. But if something could be done, action was taken.

With old age, one eventually became a burden upon the camp—one could not be productive, yet one required caring by others. This burden would cause hardship upon the group. By the process of *ajurnarmat* a decision was made that something *could* be done to alleviate the burden: suicide. Suicide was an honourable way to die because it acknowledged the importance of other camp members and their need to survive without unnecessary burdens. Further, suicide had a dimension of self-realization: physically the individual was no longer capable of providing for survival, but spiritually he or she was ready to accept the challenge of death. Suicide was not a desperate and irrational act. Rather, it was carefully considered and accepted.

The most common method of suicide among the elderly was strangulation by a sealskin rope. Very often a favourite member of the family was asked to assist. This assistance was in most cases granted without reservation. Other common methods were to walk out upon the land or ice or to ask to be left behind by a travelling group and thereafter die of exposure or starvation. The remaining members of the family grieved at the death of a loved one but accepted it as a necessary part of life. So, here we see *ajurnarmat* providing strength to individuals and families at times of greatest challenge and profound grief.

In times of mental depression, such as created by a serious personal crisis, suicide could be an alternative course of action, but it was dependent upon several conditions and choices. It was first of all an individual decision arrived at after much spiritual thought and many efforts to discuss the depression with other camp members. If an individual could not resolve their depression and thus felt themselves a burden upon the group or experienced an unresolvable desire to free their personal soul from bodily confinements, this individual could quite legitimately "will" suicide. Again, this was an honourable death, for the Inuk had struggled within to determine his or her own fate, and through this struggle had decided upon a course of action for which they took responsibility. Death by suicide, or any other cause, gave freedom to the soul.

Summary and Conclusion

The physical survival of the Inuit group depended upon camp harmony and cooperation, and those who interfered with the harmony or could not provide towards the survival of the group were allowed an honourable exit. The philosophy of the Inuit allowed suicide as an acceptable death, not only individually but for the greater survival of camp members. The belief system, philosophy and physical environment all joined in a harmonious balance towards searching and understanding, with the ultimate benefit being that of the group and the development of a group consciousness. An understanding of these factors is critical to a comprehension of the highly complex personal relationships found within an Inuit group.

Chapter 2

The Social and Psychological Survival of the Group

The social and psychological elements of Inuit culture include the family structure, the general training that takes place among the children, the behaviours that result from this training, and the mind processes that result from cultural pedagogy. The processes of mind result in language and influence the construction of that language. For example, the English language is linear, but many Native languages are circular. The language ultimately results in the transmission of the culture, whether through art, music and dance, or oral tradition. It is critical to understand that once the language has been replaced, transmission of the culture becomes exceedingly difficult, if not impossible.

The Inuit have been able to retain much of their language and family structure, allowing an understanding and acceptance by the children of the ways and practices of their parents and those to whom the care of the children is entrusted. The social and psychological survival of the Inuit has depended upon two factors: (1) the relationships within the group and (2) modes of helping that were culturally designed and acceptable. Relationships, particularly those found in families and partnerships, and cultural rules assisted the Inuit in maintaining group harmony. Some of the thought patterns of the Inuit provide an insight into traditional helping skills and the techniques employed to ensure the effectiveness of those skills.

Relationships

The most consistent formal relationships within Inuit groups are found in a very complicated network of *affinal* (i.e., marriage) *bonds* (*ilagiingniq aipparmigut*) and *consanguineal* (i.e., blood) *bonds* (*ilagiiniq angajuqqaatigut*) that is further complicated by partnerships. Three basic factors are at play in Inuit relationships: (1) collaboration, i.e., partnerships for securing food supplies and basic survival, (2) kinship, including consanguineal and affinal ties found in extended family networks, and (3) designated dyadic relationships within the nuclear family.

Among the Inuit, the emphasis upon relationships allowed cooperation and assistance without mistrust or guilt. Group cooperation was the basis of physical survival, within which a complex system of kinship terminology clearly specified the relationship and responsibility of the individual to the group. The word or phrase used to refer to or address another Inuk described a relationship between individuals. For example, a male child given the name Okina would be called by many names by those with whom he had a relationship. For example, Okina would be called "little brother" by his older sister and "older brother" by his younger sister, "my husband" by his wife and "my son" by his father. Or he might be referred to by others as "my brother's son" or "my wife-exchange partner." This use of relationship designations in speech was valuable in efforts that required collaboration, for when one Inuk addressed another, each was reminded of the duties in their relationship.

> In these circumstances of arctic life, Inuit were able to create and maintain intensive relationships with each other that made possible, and in fact demanded, close co-operation. As occasion demanded they also seem to have been able to temporarily suspend such ongoing relationships and to effectively establish new and intensive social relationships by a variety of means (Guemple 1976, 182).

Partnerships

One of the most effective relationship patterns was partnerships.

> In those days, if you had a partner, it was just like having a relative, a brother-in-law or a sister-in-law. I would save a special part of any animal for my partner. No one else would get that part (Luke Iqallaq, as quoted in Freeman 1976).

Partnerships were strengthened by a complex yet highly effective system. Seal-sharing partnerships described by Van de Velde (1956) provide a clear example. Shortly following the birth of a male child, his parents would approach parents of other male children to seek out prospective partners for their child. Upon agreement—based on the similar likes, dislikes and hunting strengths of the fathers—a partnership would be struck for the male children whereby, when they reached manhood, they would, in a strict sense, be partners for life. The design of this partnership was based upon the parts into which a seal was traditionally divided, and the names used between the partners corresponded with their part of seal. For example, one boy would be called; after the head of the seal, Nait'ok, while the other was the rear, Okpat, and the two would refer to each other from earliest childhood by these names, reminding themselves of their affiliation. When they became hunters, the partnership was not dependent upon hunting together as a unit, but rather it required them to share food. Okpat, having caught a seal, was bound by the rules of the group to give Nait'ok the head; and, likewise, Nait'ok was bound to give Okpat the rear (ibid.).

Men provided the physical needs for the group, including food, shelter, skins for clothing, and household materials and utensils. Should a hunter die or become disabled, the partnership rules insured that his family would be provided for by his seal-sharing partners.

Spouse-exchange partnerships further guaranteed care of the family should the husband be unable to provide. The male exchange partner became responsible for the provision of food and shelter to the women with whom he had united, and the children born of those women. The spouse-exchange partner might also be a hunting partner, but in many cases was not. The importance put upon the spouse exchange was as great as that put upon the hunting partnerships.

Partnerships were essential for the physical and psychological survival of the group. The responsibilities and rules were defined, and breach of these resulted in severe treatment.

Extended Family

> A family cooperative that would stick together through good times and bad, succor or come to the defense of their own blood kin and even seek vengeance on anyone who harmed any member of their clan ... here was the security that the individual lacked. Within this group he could move freely for his extended family was, so to speak, the inner keep of a fortress which protected him from any attack or adversity aimed at him by the outside world (Hebert 1976, 34).

After Rasmussen had travelled the Arctic region in 1924, he wrote of the pronounced *group communalism (piqutiqaqatigiingniq)* he found in the Inuit camps. Boas (1888), Jenness (1928) and Freuchen (1961) all comment upon the communal accommodations found in the camps, particularly during the cold and dark season. The cooperative efforts of the Inuit are further demonstrated in their hunting practices and their adherence to strict rules governing the distribution of meat, as noted by Balikci (1970), Rasmussen (1931) and Van de Velde (1956). Briggs (1970) reports some lack of cooperative sharing among the Utku, but from my own experience and knowledge of the same people with whom Briggs resided, I would question her comments in this regard. One need only recall the famine of 1957-58 to verify the value placed upon communal attitudes within the group. This is not to say that Briggs' observation is incorrect, but the group of families of Back River at that time were not particularly homogeneous, and lack of cooperation among them could have been an indicator of social and psychological unrest.[10]

The extended family was inclusive of all members related by blood, and the most important relationship in the extended family was that of the oldest member, regardless of sex, to the oldest able hunter. According to my informants and my own observations, the eldest member of the extended family assumed the role of advisor and confidant to all other members. This role was distinguished from that of the "fatherhead," the oldest able hunter, in that the aged advisor was supposed to possess wisdom *(issuma*[11]*)* and thus have demonstrated an ability to listen carefully and respond with clear and accurate advice. The fatherhead had demonstrated and been accepted for his ability to maintain authority and to delegate responsibility for obtaining items necessary for survival.

The extended family network provided for cooperation and distribution of food and had a fair amount of flexibility despite its apparent cohesion. The extended family not only offered psychological security, friendship and acceptance but also provided an *issumatuq* (wise individual) who could be consulted on all matters. Thus the system of authority provided a built-in helper or support person who effectively reduced the emotional tensions and frustrations of the Inuit who sought their advice. The young Inuk was raised with the concept of the authority and wisdom of the elders. And the expectation that help and superior experience would be present in time of need allowed ready acceptance of that authority.

> The old saying is that an old person is wiser than a young one.
> Some older people say that the one who listens to his parents will
> live longest. If you listen to older people and are told to do

something, you will live longer and have a better life (Bernard Iquuqaqtuq at Pelly Bay, as quoted in Freeman 1976).

Nuclear Family
Within the extended family were several nuclear units and individual variations in age, experience, insight, demonstrated authority and power.

> In my first days in the qaqmaq it was during the evening when our visitors had gone home and we were preparing for bed that I felt most strongly the special warmth of the family, its closeness as a unit.... Memories of dependence, of sacrifice, of happiness, private jokes too, were threads of intimacy that I felt binding and giving security to the members of Inuttiaq's family (Briggs 1970, 79-80, 85).

The main characteristics of the traditional nuclear family included co-residence, division of labour and activity, intimacy in child rearing, and sex. This core unit provided a solid basis for strong, larger units composed of many nuclear families, each of which shared and collaborated for the benefit of the larger group. In this system, one or more families could be relatively unstable internally and yet not negatively affect, to any great degree, the well-being of the entire group. Social ties strengthened the unity of the remaining families.

Marital bonds provided the foundation of the nuclear family, and several factors combined to strengthen the initial bonding. For example, the customary division of labour and mutual interdependence of marriage partners created a complementary work force. Each became a helper to the other in their efforts to survive.

Role of Men
Early training and modelling prepared a young male child for his future role as a provider of the food and material essential for survival. As he matured, increased activity was encouraged. At the age of puberty the boy was considered old enough to hunt. The ceremony of becoming a man, and thus a hunter, took place when he caught his first seal. This ceremony provided tremendous encouragement to the young hunter, because the entire camp would gather to share and to feast upon the seal while verbally complimenting the young man.

Inuit men were responsible for inventions, particularly those related to hunting activities, that enabled the group to utilize the elements about them more successfully. Laughlin (1976) refers to ingenious devices such as the kayak, goggles and stools, and he also notes the non-material qualities such as psychological and social inventiveness that assisted in the development of the individual as a part of a group.

Nelson (1976, 203) substantiates this statement with his observations on the self-assertiveness and competence the Inuit hunters impress upon others. The Inuk was viewed as "uncommonly self-assured about his knowledge and ability to cope in any situation ... [and] equally confident of his physical competence and ability to persevere in the completion of any task." As noted by Nelson, alertness and cooperation were strong qualities in the Inuk hunter, qualities that are still found within the personality of the male Inuk, and specifically in his attitude and role in the nuclear family.

As a hunter, the Inuk male respected leadership, knowledge and cooperation. In the nuclear family, he equally respected these qualities in his wife. The role of Inuit women was as important and meaningful as his own role.

Role of Women
From earliest childhood, females were encouraged to imitate the roles of adult women. Games were a replay of the daily activities of women and centred on things such as caring for smaller children, household management, the preparation of hides for clothing or the drying of meat and fish.

The duties of women balanced those of the men. One without the other could not survive the environment. Thus, a joining together in a cooperative effort was essential.

In a comparison of two groups of Inuit, the Qipi and Utku, Briggs (1974) describes the former male group to be more passive in the home than the latter. My own field work among several groups across the Canadian Arctic also reveals the Qipi to be more representative of male-female equality in the relationship.

> Qipisa husbands are leaders only with regard to hunting and traveling; indoors, the woman is the leader. ... If men are talking together, women listen, and if women are talking, men listen. They do not ignore or depreciate each other's conversations, they listen with interest but rarely join in (Briggs 1974, 276).

The Wife and Husband Partnership
The union of Inuuk man and woman resulted in a deep, cooperative partnership that was critical to individual survival within the well-formed system of group relationships. The respect husband and wife extended to one another reached beyond cooperation for physical survival to psychological and social compatibility. My own field work has

evinced a deep caring of one for the other, and a warm tenderness expressed in touching and gentle emotivity within the seclusion of the nuclear family environment. This observation of special intimacy shared among husband and wife is supported by Briggs (1974, 277): "At home, when visiting neighbours have left and only the family is present, it is the husband and wife who . . . talk and laugh together."

Arranged marriages appear to be central in all groups of Inuit (Balikci 1970; Briggs 1970, 1974; Guemple 1976). At birth, or shortly thereafter, a child would be promised to a child of the opposite sex by the parents. My own observations reveal that a sense of acceptance emerges as two children grow to adulthood knowing they are to share their lives together. A breach of promise constituted a serious wrong, but noncompatibility after a trial marriage was regarded as an acceptable reason to void the contract.

Arranged marriages prepared children for psychological and social compatibility. This compatibility appears to have been further enhanced by several factors that Briggs (1974) also supports. Such criteria included physical dependence and cooperation, and the intimate bonds of shared experiences, struggles, fears and pains. In addition, I have noted in my field work an intense, binding strength in the respect shown for inner psychological privacy, and in the silent companionship displayed when all has been said or need not be said. The formation of the marriage bond follows a pattern of physical cooperation leading to a psychological and social compatibility built upon respect for each as an individual of equal worth. "If spouses are ill-matched, so that they do not give each other companionship and appreciation, if for some reason they cannot have children, if the man is a poor hunter or his wife a clumsy or lazy seamstress, there will be trouble" (Briggs 1974, 278).

Within the world view of the Inuit a good hunter and a good seamstress represented a strong and dependable partnership. "Which is better (or more important), a good hunter or a good seamstress, is meaningless in Eskimo; both are indispensable" (Briggs 1974, 288). However, this is not to imply that jealousy, envy, anger and other such emotions did not exist. These are adequately documented in both historical and recent reports (Briggs 1970, 1974; Balikci 1970; Rasmussen 1931; Freuchen 1961; Freeman 1976). Briggs (1974, 291) presents an excellent discussion of disparagement at an unconscious level based upon (1) a desire by men to be dependent upon women, (2) an envy of women because they remain at camp while the men struggle and endure hardships in hunting and (3) a desire for revenge upon the "scathing tongues" of women. Though Jenness (1928) uses these negative emotions as an example of male dominance over women, his arguments are presented from a white, Western world view.

To imply that difficulties did not exist within Inuit culture would be incorrect. However, these difficulties were based in the Inuit world view and thus were related to the harmony of the group within the environment. Briggs (1974) questions the extent to which there was unconscious hostility within the marriage relationship. The area of the unconscious still requires further study from an Inuit world view. At a conscious level, Briggs states:

> I see no ... institutionalized conflict among men and women and also— as societies go—relatively little unconscious potential for tension that is specifically directed by one sex towards the other. This is not to say that Eskimo interpersonal relations are free from conflict. They are full of conflict, but (to repeat) very little of the conflict seems to be institutionalized among the sexes (ibid., 300).

Role of Children

> The Eskimo has deep affection for his [sic] family. He will do and sacrifice more for his children than any people I have ever known, without exception. This kindness extends not alone to his own flesh and blood but to orphans and other dependents, who are unable to care for themselves (Whitney 1910, 129).

The procreation of children not only provided the family with joy but promised future security. The presence of a potential provider, either directly (e.g., a male child) or indirectly (e.g., the husband of a female child), created an increased probability of future stability and could be claimed as a contributing factor to good mental health. The rearing and teaching of children gave meaning to the life and struggles of the Inuit, and immense joy and happiness. Diamond Jenness (1928, 210) supports these thoughts:

> They needed children for their own happiness, to satisfy the instinct for parenthood and to support their declining years; but they needed no more than would maintain their number at an even level.

The children's early care and imitation of their parents' camp duties was followed later by strict and consistent education in matters of survival, and ultimately by responsibilities that reflected the fact that in each nuclear family the parents were the determining factor in overall survival. In the Arctic, many stories are told of entire Inuit camps being wiped out by starvation, disease or other factors. Thus, the future survival of the camp was a responsibility placed upon each parent. Traditional families valued each individual. They were strong and supportive and each member developed a sense of being accepted by, and likewise accepting, the others around him or her— nuclear family members, extended family and the entire group.

Traditional Healing

Having briefly described the Inuit's family and social relations, and the realities of their physical surroundings, we can now turn to components within Inuit culture that were involved in their traditional psychological process of helping, which effectively reduced anxiety and promoted cooperative efforts. Three factors were of overwhelming importance in the psychology of the Inuit: (1) acceptance of things that cannot be changed, (2) silent acceptance and (3) seeking and gaining advice when a matter can be changed. Application of culturally appropriate terminology will again assist the investigation.

Ajurnarmat

Throughout my work with the Canadian Inuit, I have noted the constant reappearance of one word in Inuktitut that most graciously sums up the basic philosophical attitude of this culture: *ajurnarmat*. During my contact with the traditional helping skills of the Inuit, I formulated an understanding of this concept and find that it can be summarized as follows: things are the way they are and it makes no practical sense to despair over something that has already occurred or cannot be changed.

The concept of *ajurnarmat* is not the product of a fatalistic society, but rather has emerged from among a group of people whose world view and philosophy included greater acceptance than some other cultures. Rather than being given to reflections on the past, they choose to live each day at a time and to seek the challenges of the future. Jenness (1928), Stefansson (1921, 1951), Coccola and King (1955) and many other authors provide evidence of this. All students of Inuit culture may not share my enthusiasm or agree upon the extent to which *ajurnarmat* is indicative of acceptance of things past rather than of a fatalistic attitude towards life. But my search of the literature and my field work allow me to conclude that in the Arctic the emotional and physical survival of the people absolutely depended upon getting on with living. They simply could not waste time in despair or yearning, because they were faced each day with the reality of finding food and shelter.

It was not an easy life, nor a life of constant joy. But the Inuit are not, as some authors have indicated, "God's frozen children, unchristian, unwashed and definitely inferior" (Ross, as quoted in Rasky 1976, 13). Rather, they are men and women who accomplished tremendous and ingenious feats in their will to survive and built highly effective approaches to interpersonal relations into their culture.

The ability of Inuit to accept things as they are alleviated a tremendous amount of interpersonal struggle and clarified interactions and expectations in the art of helping. Elementary metaphysical assumptions of Inuit culture are revealed when we note that any request for aid meant the requester thought there was a chance that the situation could be changed to benefit his own emotional health. The helper was invoked only to provide advice and direction, or to assist in settling whether or not a matter was *ajurnarmat*. Regardless of the outcome of any conjoint thinking, the onus of action was always upon the one requesting the help. The language used in the interaction created a powerful "expectancy affect": one was *expected* to accept matters that could not be changed and to waste neither time nor energy in grief or pursuit of the unattainable.

> Whatever their fate, it held no promise of joy, no hope of reunion with kinsmen who had gone before. The only pleasures were here and now and the wise man grasped them before they passed from his reach forever (Jenness 1928, 209).

It follows that *ajurnarmat* may provide a centre for traditional Inuit psychology and a primary basis for interpersonal relations. In all cases, whether of group or individual concern, if a matter was *ajurnarmat* it was accepted. If the matter was not *ajurnarmat*, a course of action would be determined and acted upon.

The Art of Silence: An Unspoken Presence

> Well timed silence hath more eloquence than speech.
> —Tupper, *Proverbial Philosophy.*

In traditional Inuit culture, silent acceptance of the situation was paramount in times of grief or stress. *Ajurnarmat* (here used to denote the act of employing silence) provided the individual with a way to release tensions and emotional attachments and provided the group with the knowledge that the silence of everyone else indicated concern and understanding. The background expectancy was that the matter was to be accepted and life would continue.

Cases of silent acceptance often centred about the death of a loved one. The troubled person would find themselves in the company of other individuals who would, without words, acknowledge the suffering and offer a warm and human, yet silent, companionship. The one who suffered was expected to bear through the hurt, come to accept the matter and then continue on, having gained new insight and strength by virtue of having overcome grief. It was not necessary for an Inuk to explain grief or to invite others to enter into a discussion of grief. Rather, within the comradeship of silence, the group support strengthened the grieving individual to accept and then to move forward, all the while not burdening the group, and thus strengthening the prospects for group survival. What is critical here is that the group assisted the individual. The struggle was a group struggle and a group effort to heal.

> At best, Utku consider questions boorish and silly (Briggs 1970, 3).

Although Briggs limits her comments to the Utkuhikhalingmiut, my investigations reveal that the way of silence prevails among Inuit throughout the Canadian Arctic. It is perhaps a sad admission that among white North American groups silence has become an uncomfortable space. Note the discomfort experienced by one white field worker unaccustomed to silence:

> The lengthy visits of Nilak and his wife to my tent were always a misery to me. Not yet aware of the friendliness of silence, I could only sit woodenly smiling, with chilblained fingers tucked into my sleeves (ibid., 61).

Traditionally, the inner person was the only space of privacy for the Inuit, given the small size of their physical accommodations. A silent bond did not invade another's inner sanctum. Rather, it allowed an individual to feel the warmth of friendship, to grow in security with concerned individuals about them and yet enjoy personal space. When asked a question about the nature of friendship, an elderly Inuk said to me, "Good friends are those who are comfortable in silence."

In the course of my investigations, I have discovered that the present-day Inuk has, for the most part, retained a high respect for silence. Silence is used in matters requiring the acceptance of grief or hardship, and *ajurnarmat* is still a principle variable — if a course of direction can change a matter, a helper may still be requested.

Issumatuq: The Traditional Helper

Issuma is an Inuit concept somewhat comparable to "the ability to reason." However, this concept goes far beyond the common Western notion of reasoning. Issuma includes a social and group consciousness, taking into account all skills, knowledges and social and environmental influences and relationships. The concept is based on the assumption that once an individual progresses beyond childhood, he or she is able to comprehend a situation. This allows a very direct approach and alleviates lengthy and unnecessary discussions. The Inuit do not waffle about verbally. A direct statement of fact is expected to be met by an equally direct response. The response may be an answer, silence or amai ("I don't know").[12]

Briggs (1970, 358) provides an excellent analysis of the concept of issuma (which she calls ihuma):

> The concept is central in two senses. First it is invoked to explain many kinds of behaviour and, secondly, it is an important measure of the quality of a person.

Although Briggs admits that she has not fully grasped the concept, she definitely raises a number of important questions. In my experience, issuma is an acquired skill that comprises the ability to comprehend and set facts in proper order so that some understanding may be had of a situation. As one grows older, one's issuma may become an appealing characteristic to other camp members, who will then seek one's counsel.

An issumatuq (wise individual) is sought out for advice and counsel. Issuma may be said to be the gaining of knowledge over time and experience. This concept provides some insight into the respect provided by the Inuit to the elderly. And it also provides some understanding of the respect generated towards those who were considered issumatuq and their ability to settle disputes or provide individual advice when requested.

Not all interpersonal helpers in traditional Inuit society were among the oldest members of a family. Informants consistently reported that those who helped in camp members who had a good knowledge of skills essential to life and the ability to resolve problems. These characteristics suggest adults who had demonstrated credibility as helpers and acquired skills determined necessary within the culture.

In an interview, an elderly Inuk, Katsook, made the following statement regarding the settlement of disputes:

> It was not rare to have an older person intervene. In such a situation one would be chosen by either the individual/

individuals incurring difficulty or, if he/she/they did not act, a person would be chosen by camp elders to assist in the matter. The role of this helper was to listen carefully to all sides of the disagreement. A very direct approach was employed and it often occurred that just the talking out of the problem would result in the matter being resolved. If a solution was not arrived at in this manner, it was then up to the arbitrator [*issumatuq*] to determine a course of action (Pangnirtung, October 3, 1979).

This statement provides some understanding of the processes of helping that have always been a component of Inuit culture. It also provides evidence that if persons were in struggle or causing an imbalance in the group, camp elders would intercede and choose a wise person to assist in settling the dispute. The facts that "this helper was to listen carefully" and "it often occurred that just talking out the problem would result in the matter being resolved" are indicators that the traditional Inuit had acquired an approach to helping that was beneficial and culturally appropriate. The statement also provides some insight into the respect generated to the wise person, in that "if a solution was not arrived at ... it was then up to the arbitrator [*issumatuq*] to determine a course of action."

These comments have been verified by elderly Inuit in many interviews across the Arctic coast and the Baffin regions of the Northwest Territories. There was, and to some extent remains, a traditional approach to helping, and this approach is based primarily upon the acquired skills of older Inuit. Those skills include the ability to listen intently. My observations at hundreds of meetings in the Arctic have always left me amazed at the patience of the Inuit to listen totally until a speaker is finished, and even then to wait to ensure the speaker does not have an afterthought. Another skill observed by myself many times, and confirmed by many elderly and younger adults, is the ability to ensure that oneself, the listener, has understood. Rather than assuming they have understood, Inuit will often repeat the matter related back to the speaker. If the listener has not understood, he or she may also say nothing, waiting for further explanation.

A further critical skill is that of advice giving. It takes a confident and respected helper not only to provide advice but to have the advice followed. The presence of an approachable helper in each family provided a resource for discussion and guidance. If this was not acceptable to an individual, an alternate helper would be selected by the camp elders.

The individual helper was chosen for his or her maturity, which is an additional implication of the concept of *issuma* discussed earlier. But the responsibility was always upon the individual to accept the matter as it was or to determine a course of action (*ajurnarmat*). When the individual chose neither to follow advice nor to accept the trauma in silence, the results were swift and clear. Depending on the seriousness of the disharmony to the camp, several actions or punishments would be enforced. The most serious result was murder. The murder would usually be performed by two relatives of the individual causing the disharmony, so as not to invoke a family feud and cause further disharmony. The individuals who were to carry out the murder were chosen by the elders of the camp. There was no thought of refusal, for all knew that if the matter was not settled the whole camp could perish.

Perhaps the most recent case of cultural murder took place in the Spence Bay area in July 1965. It is known as the case of Soosee and involved a group of Inuit in an isolated area. Soosee apparently had suffered for years from destructive and psychotic behaviour. In July 1965, while at the camp, Soosee became violently out of control. The camp members bound her, but she broke free from the bindings. The people then attempted to abandon her, but she again broke loose of bindings before they could get safely to an island. The people were terrified of Soosee and her spirits. They were afraid she would put the madness into each of them. The matter was discussed by the leaders and it was decided that Shooyoot and Aiyaoot, two young men, would carry out the execution. Both men made several warning shots, but Soosee continued to come closer. Then they both shot at her at the same time, so neither would know who killed her.[13]

My informants in the Arctic have related many stories of cultural murders carried out for the safety and well-being of the camp. The arrival of the courts and the Royal Canadian Mounted Police (RCMP) has, of course, changed this aspect of traditional culture.

Other methods were used to ensure that individuals took the responsibility of re-establishing camp harmony when they were advised to do so. These punishments included (1) abandonment and (2) ignoring the individual. With abandonment, the person would be forced to leave the camp forever and make their way to another group, struggling alone on the way against the harsh rigours of the Arctic climate. Or the individual would be simply left behind when the group moved on to a new area. As in the case of Soosee, when a person refused to be left behind, firmer and more permanent action was taken. When an individual was to be ignored, the whole camp would act as though the person did not exist. No one would respond to the person or indicate that he or she was visible. After several days of such imposed loneliness and non-existence, most took the advice seriously and followed it, thus restoring harmony to the camp.

Brody (1975) suggests that attributing the possession of *issuma* to the elderly was a factor in their successful ability to make decisions that would be accepted by the other members. For the Inuit, *issuma* removes the need for a great deal of unnecessary discussion, gets to the core of the matter at hand quickly and without confusion, and avoids embarrassment and greater anxiety.

Summary and Conclusion

Some aspects of Inuit culture have been investigated, in particular family groups and some behaviours that resulted from learning within the culture. The roles of family members were explored, as were some of the rules within the culture. The thought pattern of the Inuit was explored, particularly through the concepts of: *ajurnarmat*, the determining factor in choosing a course of action in order to decrease stress and emotional frustration within traditional Inuit culture; silent acceptance if a matter could not be changed; and the consultation of an individual possessing *issuma* if a change was considered possible. Awareness of these metaphysical and psychological "facts" among the Inuit and an appreciation of the complexity of their relationships is of vital importance for those who would train helpers to work among this people.

Some of the techniques to ensure that the transmission of the culture took place, such as the methods to ensure that advice was taken, were also discussed. The family network and partnerships were, and to some degree remain, a critical focus for the physical and psychological survival of the group.

Although cultural transitions have brought many changes, the practice of silent acceptance and of strong respect for the elderly appear to remain within the culture as essential components in the art of helping, along with strong family ties. These general approaches, endemic to Inuit culture, have been tested by time and reality. They cannot be ignored and must be recognized and employed by all those interested in developing appropriate helping skills. Knowledge of traditional ways of helping are essential to a helper within Inuit culture. As cultural transition continues, it may be necessary to develop new approaches or borrow techniques from other cultures. But the traditional ways must remain the foundation of any innovations made to helping among the Inuit.

Chapter 3
External Influences upon Inuit Culture

A number of events have taken place in the past sixty years in the Canadian Arctic that have greatly influenced the traditional helping approaches and especially the spiritual beliefs of the Inuit. This chapter will focus on some of those events and the intruders responsible for them. The role and influences of some of the missionaries will also be discussed. I have chosen to provide accounts of two settlements particularly influenced by missionaries; the contents of of these narrations were related to me in detail by the survivors of the events, and I was asked by my informants to convey them.

Intercultural Influences
In the late 1500s, European cultures began to affect the Arctic. Events unfolded in the following sequence.

Whalers
The first recorded contact between the Inuit and European cultures appears to have occurred as a result of whaling expeditions off Baffin Island around 1590. In the early seventeenth century, whaling activity was halted because of severe ice conditions and high costs. In the nineteenth century, activity resumed, particularly around Pond Inlet (1820) and Cumberland Sound (1840) (Millard 1930; Crowe 1974; Bruemmer 1971). Initial contacts between the Inuit and the whalers were harmonious, and there was considerable trade for items each group viewed as valuable to its survival. The Inuit offered fresh meat, clothing

and ivory and they received biscuits, clothing, knives, rope and other items (Crowe 1974).

Exchanges continued for some years, and the Inuit, who believed that elements of nature such as animals, land and sea were free to all, offered no objection to European whaling activities. From these contacts came two distinct results. First, the whalers carried with them diseases and microbes foreign to the Inuit and, having no resistance to these alien germs, the Inuit became plagued with disease. It is estimated that one-third of the Inuit population had died by 1900 as a result of infection and epidemics of influenza and tuberculosis (ibid.). The second result was the depletion of wildlife as the whalers hunted for food and furs. This drop in animal populations was significant enough to result in migrations of Inuit to new hunting areas (ibid.).

Thus, early European contacts had major negative consequences for Inuit culture. Though relatively few groups actually encountered the whites face-to-face, the secondary effects of disease and famine had an extraordinary and widespread impact. It is not recorded that the whaling men were steeped in or even interested in cross-cultural awareness. For the Inuit, however, expectations had now been established about what other white men would bring.

Explorers and Fur Traders

Following the whalers, the next group of white men to visit the Canadian Arctic were either explorers (Back in 1833, Boas in 1888 and Rasmussen in 1929) or itinerant fur traders (Graham in 1744, Radford and Street in 1756, Pearce in 1790 and Finlayson in 1829). Of course, many explorers and traders roamed the Arctic and those noted above represent but a handful.

A primary result of Inuit involvement with European whalers, explorers and traders was that the Inuit became providers of services, as guides, interpreters and peacemakers—some of whom were the children of joint relationships, primarily between Inuit women and white fur traders. Many of these offspring played a vital role in the expansion of the fur trade (for example, Tatanaoyuk, born in 1795; Albert One Eye, born in 1824; and William Ouligbuik, born in 1831). Such people bridged a cultural gap. They were accepted by the people as Inuit, but they had been educated in the culture, history and languages of their European heritage.

During this second period of activity, cross-cultural contact mainly occurred around trade and barter. The literature does not indicate traders made any effort to become involved in the art of helping on a psychological level, nor is this a recorded characteristic of any of the mixed-blood,

Inuit-white interpreters. It is recorded, however, that the interpreters did act as peacemakers, but this was solely to enhance trading relationships and not to encourage group harmony for any other reason (Crowe 1974; Ayaruaq 1968). Although some of the itinerant traders did possess a lay knowledge of white medicine and helping, no evidence is available to substantiate serious efforts to extend this knowledge to the Inuit (Crowe 1974).

In most cases, the later establishment of trading posts was a part of the enterprising activities of the Hudson's Bay Company. However, Revillon Frères also set up posts in the upper Hudson Bay region. The managers of these posts often brought with them a knowledge of modern medicines.

Transient Oblate Missionaries
Oblate missionaries began to seek out Inuit groups in the Canadian Arctic in the early twentieth century. The Oblates lived with the people and travelled and hunted with them. The priests brought to these "transient missions" a ritualistic approach to helping and the belief in a supreme being who had powers far beyond those of any shaman. The Oblates also introduced some knowledge of modern medicine and small quantities of drugs. The critical impact of this knowledge and some of the work of the Oblates will be discussed later in this chapter.

Shipping
As missions and trading posts gained converts and customers, the frequency of Inuit contact with European sailing vessels increased proportionately. The vessels brought not only goods but doctors and more missionaries, all eager to help the "Eskimo." Throughout my studies and among my acquaintances I have found no one who recalls a single early doctor, missionary or trader who did not view these people as "primitive, lost souls." As an Oblate mission magazine had it:

> Up until fourteen years ago, paganism, ignorant, cruel and superstitious, reigned supreme. Licentiousness, thievery and murder were but commonplace. Unwanted babies were thrown out onto the snow to freeze. The same treatment was given the old and feeble, or else, feeling themselves to be a burden, they committed suicide. . . . Today warm, glowing Christianity has replaced the above state of affairs. There are over a hundred Christian Eskimos who turn all their efforts towards doing good (*Eskimo*, October 1945, 3).

A tragedy of misunderstanding occurred. These European men who early came to the Arctic viewed their expansion efforts as a mission and their personal commitments as a voluntary suffering undertaken to save the native people from the harsh realities of their life and to provide themselves with a better berth in the next. But they fundamentally failed to understand the cultural "reality" the Inuit had evolved and lived within for centuries in the Arctic. All the new arrivals were able to perceive were freezing climatic conditions, famine and an endless struggle for survival, and the Inuit culture looked inferior to the European world they had left behind. To these intruders, who were completely unable to understand the internal cohesion and human qualities that bound together this culture, so foreign to their own, the Inuit became nothing other than what whites supposed them to be. And this made it impossible for them to give any thought to the views the Inuit had about the whites. I recall a story related to me by one old Inuk woman who had been born in 1890:

> Yes, I recall the first time I saw a white man. He came in a big ship, such that I had not seen before. We called him Kappita. This man had with him a brother whom we called Nakoonuaq, the cross-eyes one. They came into our land, they were young and did not know how to survive. The ice came into the Hudson Bay and their ship could not move. The men of the ship thus stayed with our group for the winter. Kappita and Nakoonuaq remained in the home of my mother. They had no family and were far from their homeland, they had no knowledge of life and had to be taught much. We taught them our way of life. They were grateful and I believe a bit shameful that they had come in such ignorance. In the springtime they returned to their homeland. I did not see them again (Monica, personal interview, Pelly Bay, June 23, 1978).

In speaking with Inuit elderly, I have learned that this people viewed the white man as basically ignorant about methods of survival, and thus they did not consider themselves to be in need of the white man's help. Whites who did not understand or appreciate Inuit cultural adaptations to Arctic conditions viewed them as poor, helpless people. But this was not the Inuit view. In fact, to the Inuit it was the white men who were inept and required care. The Inuit had tested their skills and means of physical and psychological survival over generations. But these skills and approaches were unknown or undervalued by the intruders. What emerged was a mutual failure to perceive the strengths in each other's culture.

But of tremendous importance is the fact that in order to survive in the Arctic the white men required the stores of knowledge peculiar to Inuit culture, while the Inuit did not at all require European knowledge or customs to survive. But the intruders brought with them their knowledges and factors of comfort that they thought necessary for their own well-being, with little regard for the effects these efforts would have upon the Inuit. And these knowledges were pressed upon the Inuit by ignorant Europeans. Although a wide variety of white men were involved in influencing the Inuit, I shall concentrate upon the missionaries because a grasp of their role is vital to an understanding of changes that have occurred in the traditional Inuit approach to the art of helping.

Missionaries

At about the same time that trading posts were established, missionaries began to formally organize missions. The distinction between an "organized mission" and a "transient mission." as set out by the Oblates, was that organized missions had a building for use as both church and living quarters (J. L'Helgouach, personal correspondence, February 7, 1979).

In 1771 an interesting development took place on the Labrador coast where the Moravian mission had established trading posts in an attempt to teach the Inuit techniques of survival. The missionaries supposed that by being directly in control of the fur trade that some of the Inuit were beginning to rely upon, they could exert power over the Inuit and gradually introduce them to European customs and beliefs. However, the outcome of their efforts proved contrary to their expectations, for the actual result was an increased dependency of some Inuit upon whites and a shattering of the traditional lifestyle (Hawkes 1916).

In 1912 the Oblate missionaries founded the first Catholic mission at Chesterfield Inlet. Father Turquetil (called Oomilik, "the bearded one") and Father LeBlanc (Idgalik, "the one who wore glasses") were the founders. Until 1921, this mission was vacated and occupied during alternate years. After 1921 the Oblates traversed frequently along the Hudson Bay and Arctic Ocean coasts, opening missions in Southampton (1926), Eskimo Point (1928), Igloolik (1929), Coppermine (1929), Repulse Bay (1932), Bathurst Inlet (1935), Pelly Bay (1936), Cambridge Bay (1937) and Holman Island (1939) (Freeman 1976; J. L'Helgouach, personal correspondence, February 7, 1979; Lionel Ducharme, personal correspondence, March 10, 1979). The Baffin Roman Catholic missions opened in 1930 at Pond Inlet and in 1938 at Cape Dorset. Later, missions were opened in Perry River, Gjøa Haven and Spence Bay. The dates marking the official foundation of the Catholic missions coincide with the dates when a permanent building was erected. Previously the missionaries had travelled in the area and usually lived in a tent with a group of Inuit (L. Ducharme, personal correspondence, March 10, 1979).

In the Coppermine area, Fathers Rouviere and Leroux travelled among the Inuit for two summers from 1911 to 1913. In 1913 these priests were murdered by two Inuit, Sinnesiak and Uluksak. This case prompted one of the first murder investigations in the Canadian Arctic and illustrates the acute lack of cultural understanding demonstrated by the two missionaries. From accounts given by Inuit, one of the priests had used physical force upon the two Inuk guides and demanded that both men proceed with them cross-country in storm conditions. The Inuk thought it best to remain in camp until the weather had improved. The priestly use of force and threats by a rifle caused the Inuk to fear for their lives and they murdered the two priests in self-defense and retaliation (RNWMP 1916, 1917-18). What is most difficult to understand is not the murder but the failure of the white men to trust the judgement of those who knew the country and upon whom they were utterly dependent.

Anglican missions began as early as 1894 in the Blacklead Island area. Later, this particular mission moved to Pangnirtung, where in 1928 the Anglican mission operated a hospital. Anglican missions were also opened in Lake Harbour (1909), Aklavik (1919), Coppermine (1928) and Pond Inlet (1929). Later missions opened throughout the Arctic as communities grew (L. Ducharme, personal correspondence, March 10, 1979).

Analysis of mission opening dates reveals that the Anglicans tended to move in only after missionaries or companies were present. But Roman Catholics, of whom most were Oblate priests, tended to travel with the Inuit, live upon the land with them and blend into their culture. Rather than having the Inuit come to them, the Oblates tended to go to the people. This approach gave the Oblates a greater understanding and appreciation of Inuit culture than the Anglican missionaries who attempted to press their own culture, morality and values upon the people.

Several cases are recorded of Oblate priests being the only whites among an Inuit group: Father Henry lived alone among the Inuit in the Pelly Bay area in 1935, Father Van de Velde was the only white among the Arvilinghuarmiut[14] until 1961, Father Duplain resided with the Inuit of the West Hudson coast, and Father Ducharme travelled in various areas with the Inuit. I could find no evidence of an early Anglican missionary being the only white among a group of Inuit except for short periods. It is probable that these different approaches of the Christian groups resulted in differing levels of acceptance, and perhaps in acceptance for different reasons. While the Oblates gained entry to the Inuit culture by initiating an air of mutual respect, the Anglicans relied more on strong preaching and a firm and fiery application of the Bible. The results for the

Inuit are well portrayed in the histories of two settlements—Sanikiluaq and Pelly Bay—that will be analyzed later.

Missionary Influences

The Christian missionaries threatened the role of the shaman, and there appears to have been an early psychological rivalry between the two. This rivalry consisted primarily of mutual denigration of one another's powers, along with continual backbiting. The most common mode of conflict recorded seems to have been as follows: representatives of each side would gather together in separate settings and criticize the opposed group and leader, instilling a fear of association with them among their own group (*Eskimo*, 1943-54; Balikci 1970). But with the increasing arrival of the *qallunaaq*, shamanism went somewhat underground.

Despite the apparent victory of Christianity, informants tell me that shamans are still consulted, though this is always a very private affair. I am equally aware that this centuries-old tradition is fading fast as the youth become more intrigued with *qallunaaq* society and accepting of *qallunaaq* religions.

The initial contact had missionaries, literally without invitation, moving into traditional Inuit camps and setting up residence. To understand Inuit acceptance of such intrusions, it is helpful to consider several variables. First, the missionaries, particularly the Oblates, Moravians and to a lesser degree Anglicans, were men who, although they did depend upon the Inuit for survival, could assist in hunting and fishing and did so actively. Second, the missionaries were avid learners who expended tremendous energy studying the Inuit culture and applying their understanding. The missionaries, especially the Oblates, participated in hunts, travelled rigorously in the Arctic and fully assisted in camp life. They introduced some of the first medicines and continually cared for the ill in times of famine and epidemic. They learned the language and customs very quickly and, initially at least, took care not to break with prevailing ways. All of these actions made them initially acceptable to the Inuit, just as these missionaries might have endeared themselves to anyone else. The fact that all of the first missionaries were men was a benefit in a hunting society. And most of these missionaries could keep up with the strongest of the Inuit.

The period of introduction and transition to Christianity varied greatly throughout the Arctic. However, the persuasive efforts of the missionaries have affected every Inuk alive. I do not know of any Inuk who does not profess himself to be a Christian. It is amazing, when one considers the vast expanse of the Arctic and the difficulties of travel, that these men so convincingly changed the traditional beliefs of a people in such a relatively short time. In some cases, contact with the missionaries may have been of great benefit to the Inuit because the group developed a more stable existence, both emotionally and physically. However, this perspective varies depending upon whom one speaks to. Some Inuit are very positive towards the activities of the missionaries, and others are equally negative. However, there are certain cases where most would agree that the results were disastrous. So the reader may appreciate these two extreme, I shall review the histories of two vastly different missionary settlements, Pelly Bay and Sanikiluaq.

Case Study 1: Pelly Bay
Pelly Bay is located at 68° latitude, 89° longitude, in the Canadian High Arctic. The first recorded contact with white people is said to have occurred in 1829 with the arrival of John Ross, and the group came in contact with John Rae in 1854. Both encounters were brief (Brice-Bennett 1976).

In 1920 the Hudson's Bay Company opened a store at Repulse Bay. This resulted in more frequent contact with the Pelly Bay Inuit as they journeyed to Repulse to barter for supplies. "The first white person to live in Pelly Bay was a Roman Catholic priest who arrived in 1935. His stone-built mission formed the nucleus of the present settlement" (ibid.). This missionary was Father Henry, an Oblate priest. During the winter of 1935, he resided in a cave on the side of a hill. In 1936, Father Henry constructed a small stone church that also served as his living space. In 1938, Father Van de Velde joined Father Henry in his efforts to convert the Pelly Bay Inuit and the two men worked rigorously with the people. In 1946, Father Henry departed from Pelly Bay because of illness while Father Van de Velde remained, the only white in the community until 1961, when a school was built (ibid.; Hewett 1970; *Eskimo*, 1944-53).

From the standpoint of the Oblates, the mission was a tremendous success. The events recorded in the Oblate newsletter, *Eskimo*, verify that by the 1950s many of the Pelly Bay people had been baptized and were practicing Christians. Clabaut (*Eskimo*, December 1952, March and June 1953) provides excellent information about these conversions and the competition that developed between the shamans and the missionaries. Clabaut notes cases of illness where, after the powers of the shaman had failed to provide a recovery, the priest would be requested to assist. Both Father Henry and Father Van de Velde possessed medical knowledge and were able to apply their skills, often with success.

The following is one case that is typical of several recorded (*Eskimo*, 1943-54): Etenar was a middle-aged man whose wife Welik was partially blind. This was critical as she could neither prepare the skins nor sew the clothing essential for life in that climate. Etenar and Welik had visited the shaman, but his powers could not improve her sight. Finally, Etenar approached Father Henry, and an ultimatum was put to the priest. "We came to 'follow' (your religion). But you know that my wife is practically blind, unable to make our moccasins. We have no seamstress. If only you could cure her, all of us would follow" (*Eskimo*, 1943, 5). The priest told Etenar that he would put an ointment on Welik's eyes and they would then all join in prayer. Father Henry realized the stakes were high. The ointment was applied, the eyes were bandaged and for nine days the group prayed and sang for the recovery of the woman's sight. On the ninth day, the bandage was removed and to the surprise of everyone the woman announced that she could see and would be able to sew. The following day several Inuk were baptized (*Eskimo*, June 1953).

This example demonstrates competition between the missionaries and the shamans. The significant variable was that the shamans did not have knowledge of Western pharmacopoeia, upon which the missionaries were able to capitalize to strengthen their influence.

Study of traditional approaches to mental health indicates that most cultures have relied upon the combined effects of pharmacopoeia and culturally relevant concepts of helping (Asuni 1975, Marsella 1979). However, Canadian Inuit culture is unique in that the traditional approach was exclusively psychosocial; there is no evidence of pharmacopoeia (Minor 1979; O'Neil 1979). Although Lantis (1959) reveals evidence of the combined approach among the western Alaskan Eskimo, no recorded evidence of this type exists for the Canadian Inuit. Thus the missionaries of the Canadian Arctic were in a uniquely advantageous position to impress members of the other culture with their medical knowledge. Their successes in this area were crucial to the creation of positive attitudes towards them and to the eventual following of their religious preaching among the Inuit.

Having gained the confidence of the group, the missionaries never failed to offer their own religious beliefs as the explanation for positive changes. Again I cite an example from Clabaut:

> Many strange things were happening in the camp, there were unexplainable noises and animals appearing and disappearing. The camp was very uneasy. One day the entire camp became upset when they saw a man sitting on the iglek (sleeping platform). The Inuit were terrified, they thought it was the devil. Father Henry was called and he went to the tent. When he arrived at the tent it was vacant, he blessed the home and departed. Upon returning to the mission he advised the group "you can go back now, the Sign of the Cross has chased the devil away (*Eskimo*, June 1953).

Diligent pursuit of such theatrics enabled Fathers Henry and Van de Velde to become strong leaders in the community. They gained tremendous respect, and the role of the shamans was overcome and dismissed by the efforts of these two men. Eventually every member of the camp was baptized and became a practising Catholic. The camp evolved into a permanent settlement of approximately 250 people. Until 1961, the missionary at Pelly Bay was the only white inhabitant there. Both Fathers Henry and Van de Velde were very involved in community activities.

In Pelly Bay today, the community centres around the cooperative store that Father Van de Velde assisted in starting. All social services in the community are provided by community members, with the exception of three or four white teachers and one white nurse. The people continue to rely upon seal, char and caribou for food. It is an active and self-sufficient community. Welfare payments are minimal and a strong sense of community responsibility is maintained. Pelly Bay people are emotionally and psychologically strong. They view their religion as a serious activity but are also very practical. Maintaining a kind of consistency with their own traditions, religion is viewed as part of their lives, but it does not completely control their lives. Having spent time in almost every major settlement in the Canadian Arctic, I find that Pelly Bay is the most psychologically healthy community of Inuit in the Arctic.

The Pelly Bay group has long been noted as strong and aggressive towards alien influences (Rasmussen 1931). The group quickly unified and gave recognition to Inuit who were believed to possess *issuma*. These leaders guided the group and ensured that only the positive aspects of the alien culture were encouraged to blend with the Inuit culture, and thus a strong self-sufficiency developed. The traditional strengths of the Pelly Bay group ensured that missionary influences did not destroy their well-being.

Case Study 2: Sanikiluaq
The history of Sanikiluaq is sketchy at best. The first recorded involvement between *qallunaaq* and Inuit on the island is dated September 30th, 1919, and occurred out of the police investigation into the murders of Ko-Okyuk and Ketauskuk (RNWMP 1919).

The investigation by Inspector Philips revealed that the men were murdered following a public acclamation that they were social deviants and considered harmful to the community. Thus, the matter had been discussed by the elders of the group and a decision had been made: both men were to be killed for the benefit and well-being of the group as a whole. The duties were assigned to relatives of the men and the murder were carried out. Though no charges were made by the outside author ties, the results of the interference provided by the investigation would return to haunt both the whites and Inuit, and to challenge the sanity and tranquility of Sanikiluaq.

Following a twelve-day tour of the Belcher Islands, Inspector Philips returned to Ottawa in mid-October 1919. There he filed a report stating that the Inuit of the Belcher Islands were so in need of the basic requirements of survival that every effort should be made to help them. He described the Inuit as dressed in the skins of dogs, birds and seals. The people appeared physically undernourished and displayed the mental characteristics associated with starvation (RNWMP 1919). As noted in the roughly kept death records from that time, from 1919 until late 1960, many deaths were reported among young children as a result of poor nutrition. As recently as 1978, two dead women were brought in from the camp and were recorded as having perished of starvation (Health and Welfare Canada 1919-80); Canada 1918-80; Northwest Territories 1965-80).

On the Belcher Islands the food supply of the Inuit consisted of seals and ducks. There has been no trace of caribou except in one quarry, discovered in the 1970s, that contained the bones of a caribou herd. This herd is thought to have migrated from the mainland and become lost upon the sea ice, eventually ending up on the Belcher Islands. How the entire herd died or was killed has not been determined. This absence of caribou makes the Belcher Islands people unique as an Inuit group. However, artifacts and oral history provide evidence of the survival of the group upon the islands for several centuries.

Although by Western standards or even those of other Inuit groups, the Belcher Islands people continually existed on the very edge of starvation, they did survive for generation after generation. The harsh Arctic climate they faced demanded stamina and strength. The oral history and mythology of the group provide evidence of strengths of endurance and character among some of the people over the passage of time. Informants stated that the original people of Sanikiluaq were a group who lived in sod houses and had "little Inuit sense of mind." They were considered by others to be "an ignorant group," incapable of grasping or formulating ideas. They are described as "cave people," and it has been pointed out to me that in Sanikiluaq today some people of little "sense" or "thought" are still present within the community. They "appear as normal Inuit but are unable, in their own minds, to form opinions or make decisions." Informants reported to me that "the group of little sense is equal in number to those considered normal."[15]

From the arrival of the Royal North-West Mounted Police (RNWMP) in 1919 to the present day, Sanikiluaq has at times been submerged in mystery and an air of paranoid fear. Upon his return to Ottawa in 1919, Inspector Philips made note of the pitiful conditions of these people, but for the most part his recommendations went unheeded. However, a Hudson's Bay trading post was started in the early 1930s and an Anglican missionary based in Great Whale River then commenced activity in Sanikiluaq. The Anglican missionaries would travel to Sanikiluaq twice a year, in spring and fall, when ice and water conditions in Hudson Bay were suitable for such a journey. A missionary would remain among the people for a four- to six-week period and then return to the mission in Great Whale River. These missionaries were totally fluent in Inuktitut. They fervently and zealously preached the Gospel at Sanikiluaq and were greatly given to the esoteric and dramatic aspects of Christianity (Price 1970; Minor 1980a, 3).

In November 1939 several residents of the island observed a tremendous meteor shower. Among the onlookers was a woman known as Mena. She viewed this display as a forecast of events to come. Shortly later, Mena heard of the efforts of Charlie Quyerak and Peter Sala to convince the people of the imminence of the second coming of Christ. At this time, Mena was camped on one island while Charlie Quyerak and Sala were on another island some distance away. Mena decided to travel to the other camp. Upon her arrival she found the entire group caught in the frenzy of what may be called a revitalization movement,[16] which had been triggered by an interpretation of the star shower in November through the much studied scriptures.

At this time, Sala and Quyerak were among the most respected men in the group. Capitalizing on this position, they became the leaders of an effort to organize a religious cult. In their preaching they insisted that the glorious astronomical display prophesied the second coming of Christ, and that Christ would arrive in Sanikiluaq among this very group. Each day from November 1939 to March 1940 this prophecy was repeated with increased emotion, and the entire camp was caught up in the hysteria and expectation. When Mena arrived at the camp in December 1939, she immediately gave support to Sala and Quyerak. Together they formed a powerful trio.

For several months, the power and influence of the trio grew. Perhaps some in the group became frightened, and perhaps some others were not impressed. But, for most, the frenzied activity added excitement to the harsh and monotonous winter months. With the return of longer days and the warming winds of spring, the madness was rampant.

In an igloo in March the movement took an important step. For many months now the people had anxiously awaited the second coming of Christ, yet it had not come to pass. Restlessness had begun to develop and

Quyerak sensed a collective anxiety and a danger of mass hysteria within the group. At this point, it was critical that leadership be maintained.

With the entire group crowded into one igloo, Quyerak soberly announced that Jesus had arrived. He declared himself to be Christ. The majority of the group, caught in a spell of hypnosis and hysteria, showed awesome acceptance of Quyerak's statement. Maintaining this trance, Quyerak then announced that Sala was God. The hypnotic rhythm of their voices and the anxiety and the close physical confinement of the group lent power to this suggestion. Soon the suggestion was whirling about the room and pounding within the minds of all. For the first time, their struggle for survival, their bitter life of hardship, had a meaning to it. The promise of a new inner strength of being, of peace and contentment, was sensed. Confusion had vanished and the mystery was revealed before them. Here and now could be seen true reality, and all became one in this new belief. It was true that Quyerak was Jesus and that Sala was God—the two strongest and most respected members of the community.

Yet, within this whirlpool of faith, one voice dared to say "I do not believe." A child of thirteen years named Sara adamantly denied acceptance. Her words angered her own brother, Allie Appaqaq. In anger, he grabbed a stick and furiously beat her. She was ordered to sit and be quiet, but then the entire group turned angrily towards the child and beat her until she lay whimpering and dying. With one violent blow, Akiinik cracked open Sara's skull with the barrel of a 30/30 rifle. Sara lay dead amidst the madness and yet, within the hysterical sickness of the group, this death itself was a victory. Now the fight against Satan had begun, and God/Sala and Jesus/Quyerak were the leaders.

It was not long before the death of Sara began to trouble the mind of Ketosiak. He felt anger and confusion, which he displayed to the camp. Ketosiak was found to be a devil and a decision was made to murder him. Sala openly challenged Ketosiak and struck him with a harpoon. As Ketosiak lay dying, Adlaykok took a rifle and shot him dead. The "mania" continued to spread through the group. The group became one in mind and action: it was death to anyone who deviated. The victors were in ecstasy, the apostles were being formed. First there was Akiinik and now Adlaykok, and, of course, Mena who had taken the role of Mary, the mother of Jesus. The trio of Sala, Quyerak and Mena was the power and the glory and all were eager to join them as disciples. And, yet, another dared to question their power. Ikpak denied Quyerak to be Jesus. Quyerak called upon Quarak, the father-in-law of Ikpak, to kill him with a shotgun. Three times he shot into the body of Ikpak. The body lay still and lifeless as Ikpak's wife looked on, as the entire group watched. No one moved. No one made an effort to stop the madness, but each watched and gloried in the excitement, the challenge, the break from the continual and monotonous fight against starvation. Three deviants were dead. Satan had been defeated and three apostles had been chosen.

At this time, only two white men, Hudson's Bay clerks, resided on the Belcher Islands. During the months of frenzy, neither had been aware of the events in the community. This is not surprising because the Inuit were scattered in random camps throughout the Belchers and only a very few resided near the post. Each year in early March, one of the clerks would travel in the company of an Inuk guide to Great Whale River to pick up supplies and mail. Thus, on March 12, 1940, Ernie Riddell and his guide journeyed over to Great Whale. The guide was Sala. Following their arrival in Great Whale, Sala chose to confide the events in Sanikiluaq to Harold Udgarden. The story became public and a dispatch was sent to the RNWMP in Ottawa.

Riddell and Sala journeyed back to the Belcher Islands, not knowing that during their absence another tragedy had occurred. On the morning of March 29th, while other camp members had left to hunt for food, Mena had led those remaining in a religious frenzy. She had begun by running from individual to individual screaming that Jesus was coming (Jesus being Quyerak, who was away from the group at that time). The hysteria grew. The excitement was compelling, and Mena held the group spell-bound. Everyone gathered in an igloo, the group consisting of one man, six children and four women, including Mena. In hysteria, Mena led a mad dance onto the ice. Everyone followed Mena's instructions to take their clothing off except Moses Ippak and Peter Sala's wife. These two recognized the insanity about them and, each grabbing a child, fled to an igloo. Although Mena herself was not physically harmed, the remaining six were found upon the ice the following morning, their bodies naked and stiff. They were dead.

It had all gone too far. Now, not only had agents of Satan been destroyed, but the innocents too were becoming victims of this terrible madness. The camp was destroying itself. A sober acceptance of insanity replaced the jubilation and excitement. The destructive forces had reached a horrible climax. Awareness could not deny the reality of the dead women and children lying naked upon the spring ice. Sala and Riddell returned to this tragedy and patiently awaited the arrival of the RNWMP. The camp mood became one of exhausted fear and sorrow, and the pain of survival now cut to the depths of their souls.

On April 11, 1940, the RNWMP arrived and made their investigation. They departed on April 15, 1940, with Mena, Adlaykok and Quarak as prisoners, and for the next several months the anxiety of the people rose. Fear, guilt, confusion and uneasiness was experienced throughout the

Belcher Islands. This anxiety increased until August 18, 1940, when a judicial court party arrived from Toronto to proceed with charges in the matter. On August 19th, a trial commenced, with a jury composed of six white men from the Hudson Bay area. During the trial the sad story was described in detail. The law of Canada now reigned supreme among the people, and the decision of the jury was rendered: Allie Appiuaq was found not guilty, Sala and Quyerak were sentenced to two years in prison, Adlaykok was sentenced to one year, Quarak was given two years probation, and Mena and Akiinik were determined to be insane and were committed to an asylum. The matter settled, the courts and their representatives departed and the people were left behind with a broken spirit and haunting memories (Price 1970; RCMP 1921, 1941; Bruemmer 1971; Minor 1979).[17]

Conclusions

In both case examples, the extraneous influences upon Inuit culture had long-lasting effects. For example, some of the missionary influences in Pelly Bay resulted in the development of a community co-operative; however, this should not be attributed to the missionary endeavour but rather to the individual missionaries who lived in that area. Though this venture is beneficial within a Western capitalist society, it also symbolizes the changing economy among the Inuit. Rather than traditional hunting and sharing, much of the economy today centres around the co-op and a cash economy. The disharmony that resulted in Sanikiluaq is more obvious. The trauma of the early 1940s is still with the people of this community today.

The experiences of the Pelly Bay and Sanikiluaq groups leads to a clearer understanding of "how" and perhaps "why" an external influence can have such a powerful effect. Though the Pelly Bay group appears to have benefitted from some of the missionary contact, it must be noted that they have traditionally been known as a strong and aggressive group. Rasmussen (1931) particularly comments upon this and upon the abundance of food and natural resources available to the community. Balikci (1970) notes the strength of family and marital patterns, the adherence to rituals and taboos, and the complex organizational structure of the Pelly Bay group. These factors all contributed to a culturally well-adjusted band.

It may be concluded that strengths of a culture at the levels of group physical and psychological and social survival (Levels I and IIA) provide that culture with some of the power needed to withstand intruders, or to take from intruders items that will benefit the culture while rejecting aspects that are not beneficial. Pelly Bay is still one of the most traditional groups in the Arctic. With continual intrusion from outsiders, that is changing, but at a much slower rate than in most other areas. Slowing the process would allow for greater reflection and for greater retention of intrinsic cultural strengths such as the family bonds and child-rearing practices that are prevalent in Pelly Bay.

By comparison to the people of Pelly Bay, the Sanikiluaq group was ecologically marginal. Its isolation encouraged inbreeding, camp disharmony and general apathy. What could a hunter do on a small island, with no food to hunt and no means of transportation to the mainland or other hunting areas? Weakness within the culture at the group physical and psychological and social survival levels allowed cultural intrusions to take place rapidly and destructively. Though much of the traditional culture is still present at Sanikiluaq, there is also a strong Western influence, much stronger than at Pelly Bay. The overall strengths and weaknesses of a culture at the group physical and psychological and social levels thus must be considered in any analysis of external influences.

The influences of the missionaries remains strong in the Canadian Arctic. The relative effect on each Inuit group depends on the overall survival strengths within the group. Altogether, the Christian influence in the Canadian Arctic has been profound because it has removed, or at least appears to have removed, the strongly held and culturally relevant belief in the supernatural metaphysical background that supports the traditional Inuit institutions and practices of helping. Forced upon the people, Christianity is a set of beliefs with little, if any, historical or cultural relevance. Most modern Canadian Inuit no longer rely upon their own traditional beliefs in their search for spiritual satisfaction. Instead they look to Christianity. However, there is an underground shaman movement in several settlements that may encourage and interest the young Inuit. My research leads me to conclude that the Inuit have partially substituted Christianity for their earlier ideological systems. Whether this substitution is good, bad or ever helpful in the evolution and development of Inuit culture is a question that may have to be answered by the individual Inuk.

The missionaries are but one group of Arctic intruders. As noted, they were preceded by whalers, explorers and traders, each with their own agenda and most with little regard for the people of the land. These groups also had tremendous effects upon the Inuit, effects that are beyond the scope of this book. The development of shipping and trading posts also added to a disruption of the Inuit culture. But it was the missionary, and particularly the Oblate, who went in search of the Inuit with the expressed conviction of changing their beliefs. For this reason I have chosen to concentrate upon their influences and the results.

Empowering the People

Examples are many throughout the Arctic of Inuit groups applying information about their traditional culture to gain control over their own destinies. Two examples are Kitikmeot and Igloolik. In Kitikmeot, using the culture-specific design, committees were formed by representatives of the people from each settlement to advise social services. The committees called themselves Ekayuktit Nunalingna ("Helpers of the Helpers"). All social service ordinances and regulations were translated into the two dialects of Inuktitut, and many hours were spent in dialogue with each committee and at public meetings. Twice a year the entire group of about forty people from six different settlements came to Cambridge Bay to debate social service policies and procedures. The power of this group was respected at all levels of the Ministry and many changes were made. For example, these committees became the appeal committee, sat in on all hiring and made the final recommendation, advised social workers on a course of action and set up a foster home committee in Spence Bay for Inuit and Dene children requiring foster care. Committee members acted as volunteer probation officers, monitored families having difficulties and counselled persons in need. Throughout this process, traditional approaches and skills empowered the people.

In Igloolik the hamlet council has taken control of the alcohol coming into the community and of the scientists who wish to visit. After several negative experiences, the council worked out a set of rules regarding these two issues. Regarding alcohol, all requests must go through the hamlet council. No alcohol can be brought into the community unless the council approves. If persons have demonstrated responsibility in drinking, their requests are approved. However, if they cause problems in the community because of their drinking of alcohol, they are banned from ordering more for a period of time. Further irresponsibility, such as giving alcohol to a person who is restricted, results in a person's name being posted in public areas, thus employing the traditional method of public humiliation to impress upon the individual the seriousness of the matter. Scientists coming into the community to the Arctic Research Centre situated in Igloolik, must submit an explanation of their purposes to the council to gain approval.

In both Kitikmeot and Igloolik the people are demonstrating traditional problem-solving methods and an awareness of external influences. Another example of Inuit use of extraneous influences to their advantage occurred between Igloolik and Pond Inlet. Pond Inlet was considering restrictions on alcohol, and they had heard much about the experiences in Igloolik and the program put in place there. The people wanted to have a conference, but the costs were prohibitive. After discussion, they decided to set up a live television link through *Anik*. The result was that members of both communities were able to dialogue and share their wisdom and experiences, thus empowering both communities. In Pond Inlet, Igloolik and Kitikmeot, the Inuit maintain a strong cultural base.

Chapter 4
The Individual within the Group:
A View of Modern Inuit Youth

The material presented thus far allows for a clearer understanding of the traditional Inuit lifestyle, philosophy and methods of interaction. I have also highlighted some of the results of extraneous influences on Inuit culture and some of the responses to these influences. This history is critical to understanding present-day cultural transitions and the problems they bring.

Two major extraneous influences upon the Inuit have been Christianity and alcohol. These influences have resulted in lack of employment as the culture changes from a hunting-and-trading to a money-based economy. All children now attend school for at least the first few years, and thus they no longer travel with their parents to hunt during the school year. Though many youth do spend some time on the land during the summer, this experience is not sufficient for them to learn all of the traditional methods of living on the land. The school system offers them little with respect to careers, few achieve a high school diploma necessary for employment, and far fewer gain post–high school training or education. These factors, other extraneous influences and the breakdown of group physical, psychological and social survival skills have resulted in tragedy among Inuit youth.

Since the scope of this study is culturally specific helping, I have chosen to centre on present-day suicide rates, which are influenced by tradition and also by the confusions brought about by cultural changes under foreign influence.

Philosophy and Psychology

Traditionally, the role of the young Inuk was defined by sex and determined by other camp members through, for example, partnerships and
the advice of elders (Balikci 1970; Briggs 1970; Minor 1979). The characteristics and influences of the souls were accepted, but beyond this, the
spiritual search and goals of each individual were not determined by
anyone other than the individuals themselves.

Freedom and responsibility were encouraged by elders, parents and
grandparents and became internalized as a result of the requirements of
physical survival and the strong social expectations of others. The freedom provided was to develop spiritually and personally while maintaining a deep responsibility to the well-being of the camp as a whole.
Spiritual goals, of necessity, sustained a world view and provided daily
goals that encouraged good mental health. For the Inuit, physical struggles
and challenges were accepted as preparations for inner personal suffer-
ings. This combination made a relatively healthy society possible.
However, when the traditionally physical way of life was abandoned
through the intrusion of white influences and modern technology, a void
was created in personal development and the correlation of a meaningful
life with the struggle to survive became confused.

Today young Inuit are surrounded by conveniences of white society.
They have no need to hunt or to challenge the elements as their ancestors
did, nor is there any longer a pressing need to set goals or to reflect upon
their spiritual experience. There is clearly a lack of roles in comparison to
the traditional Inuit. Through a lack of traditional communal order, the
emphasis has shifted from communal responsibility to individual survival. "In fact, contemporary Inuit may be in psychological danger for
lack of clear communal roles and identity rather than for imposition of
non-native social order" (A. Stairs, personal correspondence, February
1990). Further, a growing gap between the youth and the elderly causes
an alienation of trust and a diminished desire to share. This results in
ambivalence in both parties towards mutual interaction, and thus a loss
of role models for Inuit youth. The trend becomes one towards fewer
discussions and a general unwillingness to criticize or share philoso-
phies, the struggles of life, lifestyles and influences. The youth are not
only lost in the confusing aspects of a foreign culture but also find
themselves in a cultural vacuum where the elderly are powerless to help
them.

A common psychological response among youth to this confusion is
boredom, and this boredom often leads to violence, alcoholism and
suicide. This corresponds to Frankl's (1970) discussion of loss of tradition.
As he pointed out, an existential vacuum is further increased by lack of

freedom of thought and direction. Among younger contemporary Inuit, decisions are often based upon what one "ought" to do or what one is "expected" to do rather than what one "wills" or "chooses" to do. The concept of what one "wills" or "chooses" to do was traditionally based upon inner searching and development and hinged upon individual initiative and the taking of responsibility for the group benefit. But in the modern Inuit group, emphasis is no longer placed upon self-exploration and group consciousness. Rather this challenge has given way to a vague sense of direction towards the correct course of action that white society imposes upon them through implication, technology and example. Personal responsibility for life, for which each person must answer to themselves, is taken away and individuals become objects of the social order rather than agents in its creation, objects of control rather than responsible and participating members.

In my discussions with the elderly and youth, a tremendous emotional and philosophical gulf was clearly revealed between the generations. The once strong role expectations are vanishing, the meaning of struggle is disappearing. A vacuum has been created and the attempt to fill it with material goods renders the traditional philosophy of life meaningless.

The boredom of the young Inuit appears to be a major factor in the destitution into which many have fallen. Throughout the Arctic, strong efforts are being made to supply recreational facilities, work programs and community activities, but few such efforts are successful. I recall many community feasts and drum dances that literally involved an entire settlement of Inuit. Many times these gatherings were impromptu. The elderly inevitably led the occasion, and hour upon hour the youth sat, thoroughly enthralled with the activities, taking neither a step forward nor backward. When I talked with the youth afterward, they noted a particular sadness in being unable to participate and, in many cases, being unable to understand. The youth so wish to be true Inuit, but their Levi jeans and Hudson's Bay jackets are just not strong enough to allow them this freedom. So much of what the youth depend upon takes away their Inuit culture and channels them in a direction of uncertainty.

Previously, when the traditional culture was stable, tremendous emphasis was placed upon the "will" to explore, to constantly set new goals, to become *inummariit* (a "free Inuk"),[18] whose strengths varied with the name soul but whose general characteristics included a move towards self-exploration and identity (Brody 1975). The individual was an essential member of the unit, and all struggled to perfect their lives by attaining the goals of inner contentment and harmonious communal life. It appears that these essential traditional psychological goals are being disregarded under the new influences.

The youth began as their ancestors did, their parents employing traditional child-rearing practices. However, as their society came under severe external pressure, the goals that resulted in good mental health and stable society diminished without being replaced by new ones. What remained were empty influences. The traditional psychology of the Inuit had been firmly grounded, and traditional life skills and teaching were geared, partly unconsciously, towards adaptation upon this seemingly solid ground.

Suicide and the Modern Inuit

In 1977 and early 1978 an unusually large number of suicides and attempted suicides occurred in the Canadian Arctic, resulting in a high per capita rate (CBC News; Nunatsiaq News; personal contacts and field work; Health and Welfare Canada 1979). The numbers presented a substantial increase compared to ten years earlier. For example, in 1978 the rate was 23.7 per 10,000 for the female population, whereas for the previous two years the incidence had been too small to express. Among the male population the numbers soared in 1977 and 1978 to 52.6 and 84.4 per 10,000, respectively, an increase to twice of what it had been during any past time period (Health and Welfare Canada 1979). The media, and informants directly affected, suggested various reasons for this increase.

A combination of components present in these suicides are consistent with surveys of other cultures (Klagsburn 1977). There were five primary components: (1) the majority of victims were males between the ages of 16 and 24, (2) there was a history of serious conflict, e.g.s family, judicial, or educational, in the life of the affected individual, (3) alcohol was frequently involved, (4) the individual had recently suffered the loss of a loved one and (5) the severe climatic conditions of 1978 and 1979 had made it impossible for all but a very few families to travel on the land, even during the summer. Although the influence of climatic conditions upon suicides has been disputed (Durkheim 1951; Alvarez 1972; Klagsburg 1977), this work documents the necessity for individual and group relief from the psychologically draining effects of extensive confinement in winter. During 1978 and 1979 the weather did not provide a release from the rigours of settlement life but kept people confined within their communities to an unusually high degree.

As pointed out, the depression brought on by things such as serious personal or group crisis is traditionally a motive for suicide if the psychological situation cannot be rectified. Thus, it is reasonable to suppose that suicides in the Arctic should be studied against the traditional background, and then the variable of extremely poor climatic conditions be added to account for the very drastic changes in the statistics. In a culture where experiences upon the land are an intimate part of psychology and philosophy, the absence of this vital contact during periods of extreme emotional trauma could produce severe effects. Travelling upon the land, for the Inuit, is not a holiday or retreat but rather is critical to good emotional and mental health and a direct channel towards that health. "World-image identity can be considered 'eco'-centric, in contrast to egocentric western identity, with 'eco-' comprising the social, animate and material world" (A. Stairs, personal correspondence, February 1990).

I propose that the primary causes for the increase in suicides lay in three variables, all of them interdependent: (1) emotional trauma, (2) severe climatic conditions and (3) the influences of alcohol. These three factors had the greatest effect upon young males with a history of conflict, reflecting the components summarized by Klagsburn (1977). The influences of emotion, climate and alcohol upon the vulnerable individual resulted in deadly consequences.

The variables of emotion and climate were present in traditional Inuit culture. The third variable, alcohol, is a commodity introduced only relatively recently into Inuit society. Research reveals that, prior to contact with white culture, neither alcohol nor pharmacopoeia were known to the Inuit (Minor 1979; O'Neil 1979). Alcohol is a depressant, and studies have revealed that the suicide rate among alcoholics is significantly higher than among non-alcoholics (Klagsburn 1977). Alcohol has also been shown to reduce inhibitions and give rise to a self-destructive attitude (ibid.). So, the combination of alcohol with the other two culturally present components resulted in depression and suicide.

In the case of the young Inuit, it may be that the victims were making an effort to return to a traditionally accepted and respected death. Or the burden of life may have been so great and the confusion of cultural transition so frustrating that they acted irrationally. One could argue either that suicide expresses traditional attitudes or is a result of their collapse. I am firmly convinced that there is a traditional component in most of the suicides among the youth and, further, that there are culturally specific helping approaches that are relevant and could be an aid in reducing the incidence of suicide. Some of these approaches were identified in Chapter 3 and include the use of *ajurnarmat* and *issumatuq*, silent acceptance of what cannot be changed (which does not imply an unwillingness to change those things that can be changed), to listen intently and ensure that the helper understands what is being stated, and to give advice skilfully and have it received with respect.

Spiritual Transition among Youth
Modern Inuit youth appear to be grasping for and accepting some of the traditional concepts and disregarding or failing to understand others. My field work and informants have led me to believe that young Inuit have a high regard for the art of silence and have carried this over into modern Inuit society. However, the aspect of *issumatuq*, or respect for elders, is not generally accepted as it was in the past. Some young *qallunaaq*-educated Inuit feel that the elderly do not understand their problems and thus they refuse to accept or even seek advice, even though the process of *ajurnarmat* has shown them that change must take place. Thus the very helping forces previously available for change have been cut off with no satisfactory replacement. But this is not the whole story. There are other young Inuit, who while accepting the elderly and *issumatuq*, accept the concept only because they are expected to. They do not have the genuine confidence in the elders that was part of the traditional bond between them, nor do they understand the elders' thought patterns. And there is also a small but growing group who have an appreciation and respect for the counsel of their elders and readily seek it out. For example, Josh Arreak of Pond Inlet said:

> These old people, my dad even, he doesn't know what I know. He used to learn from an old man. A real old man used to tell him things about old days and about anqaquq. My dad knows all about that stuff from one old man; every night that old man used to tell him stuff. And like, just by hearing the old man talking, you know, telling old stories and things, we get to know. I listened like that. Like I get to know a lot of things. I wish I could hear that real old man, like him talking to my dad. There's a lot of strange things, Eskimo ways and things. I guess it takes time to know these things, like I'm only 17, and I'm just learning things (Brody 1976).

The three approaches I have mentioned have vastly different results. The first approach creates a breakdown within the culture and animosity between young and old. Each becomes critical of the other and trust dissolves. In the second case, the young have expressed anger and resentment at having to accept a relationship with the elders that they lack confidence in. The elderly are aware of this and respond with anxiety. This anxiety would be expected wherever an accepted helping institution in a culture suddenly breaks down. Instead of warmth and sharing there is anxiety, distrust and a growing distance. With both the first and second approaches, the gulf between the young and old grows wider and results in information breakdown and mutual lack of under-standing. One side is ignorant of the age-old, traditional ideology and psychology, while the other is untouched by the modern concerns of the younger Inuit influenced by *qallunaaq* society. Discontent develops, and then depression on both sides. Change has moved the youth away from the elders, and it has also removed the primary traditional source of spiritual support in making change.

In the third approach there is a deep sharing and mutual struggle to understand and accept on both sides, and this generally results in good mental health and strong family bonds. Both the young and the old realize the separation of their worlds and their understandings. How-ever, though the traditional culture is now in transition, research leads me to believe that there is in this third approach a strong will among both young and old to remain in touch with the land and to preserve as much of the traditional culture as possible.

The recent increase of suicides among the youth follows from the first two approaches yet still involves the concept of *ajurnarmat*. The strong traditional child-rearing practices, which most Inuit youth were subject to, appears to have left them with some of the traditional values and psychology, but their training was not completed because of various cultural transitions. Hence, the concepts of *ajurnarmat* and silent accep-tance are well ingrained and continue to be influential in the present cultural period marked by transition.

For some Inuit, the belief in elderly *issumatuq* was strongly supported and their requests of *issumatuq* have frequently had positive results. For others, the acceptance of *issumatuq* has been lost, and thus the possibility of finding a clear channel once a decision of change is reached through the process of *ajurnarmat* has moved beyond their reach. My research leads me to believe that many younger Inuit have gone through the searching and then the painful process of deciding that change must take place, but they still remain unaware of or unaccepting of the resources available within their own culture. These modern Inuit tend to enter into a deep depression with no apparent and acceptable outlet.[19]

Traditionally, this kind of impasse was a legitimate reason to commit suicide and led to an honourable death. But now the very important aspect of *issumatuq* in the traditional psychological movement towards or away from suicide is missing. If *issumatuq* is disregarded, a crucial tool of helping has been eliminated and the helping component of community life ignored. The result is that, having decided that a change is necessary, for example, that a depression must be gotten rid of, the modern Inuk meets with uncertainty and confronts traditionally unheard-of impo-tence to act on his or her own behalf. I suggest here that when the action then taken is suicide, it is undertaken for other than clear traditional reasons; had the traditional approaches to helping been present, complete and carried out, a different and more positive result might have been effected. It is not my intention to imply that all Inuit caught in cultural transition and facing serious problems will succumb to suicide, but rather to stress that suicide may be a key issue in the development of effective helping approaches and good mental health. Further, it does not appear that the current breaks from culturally relevant approaches to "helping" are irreparable but, clearly, the development of new and appropriate approaches are critically dependent upon the Inuit themselves.

Traditional Influences
The two traditionally present components of emotion and climate helped to create situations in which suicide was not an uncommon choice. As discussed earlier, the traditional culture had developed specific ways to help a distressed or depressed individual. This approach to helping was based upon the concepts of *ajurnarmat*, silence and *issumatuq*. A decision was arrived at through the process of *ajurnarmat*, a logical approach to problem-solving where the matter was clearly considered and a decision made as to whether or not something could be done about it. If nothing could be done, it was accepted. If something could be done, a course of action was taken. When one became old and weak, one became a burden upon the camp—one could not be productive, yet required caring for, and this burden would cause hardship among the group. By the process of *ajurnarmat* a personal decision was made that something could be done to alleviate the burden: suicide.

I have no reason to believe that the way of *ajurnarmat* does not still exist for the modern Inuit. Matters still tend to be carefully considered and determinations are made that either they cannot be changed, and thus are silently accepted, or that they can be changed and a course of action is necessary. For the modern Inuit the importance of the soul-searching leading to awareness of *ajurnarmat* may have diminished in strength, and yet it is clear that the basic concept still bears directly on matters that affect the peace of mind of an individual.

An Approach to Helping
Knowledge and understanding of the traditional ways shed light upon appropriate approaches to helping among the modern Canadian Inuit. A constructive role was played by the traditional Inuit helping ways. And some of these approaches are still in practice and having beneficial effects. If non-Inuit individuals and institutions want to develop effective

means to help, it is necessary to start from the rich base provided by tradition and to modify it only to the extent that modern Inuit culture makes such modification necessary.

However, the most viable and reasonable approach is for the Inuit to develop their own approaches. These approaches would be based upon a self-determination of their needs and would most likely rely upon the traditional foundations of *ajurnarmat, issumatuq* and silent acceptance, the ability to listen intently, ensuring that the helper understands the problem, and the ability to give advice and gain respect for that ability.

Cultural Breakdown: To Recognize or to Ignore
Traditionally, the Inuit family was a strong and self-sufficient component of the social order (Briggs 1970; Minor 1979, 1980a). In recent years the family has broken down considerably (Brody 1975, 1977). Recognition of the importance of this breakdown and efforts to bridge the generation gap appear vital for the continued health of the culture. And these efforts should be primarily the product of Inuit individuals and groups working among themselves to strengthen their own culture.

Although influences and assistance may be provided by non-Inuits, the responsibility remains, and should remain, with the Inuit. It is directly in the interest of the Inuit today to take an attitude of self-determination and to develop the capabilities needed to preserve or modify their culture within the context of the strong influences of white culture in the Arctic which are impossible to ignore. Non-Inuits who wish to assist the Inuit need to appeal to the Inuit's sense of self-interest and to aid the development of self-determination, "choice" or "will" among the Inuit themselves towards the development of an approach to helping that can work in their culture today. The bonds within the culture would thus be tightened and the disempowering aspects of other cultures would be simultaneously recognized and contained.

It must be stressed that such a process cannot hope to be completed without the participation of Inuit of all generations. A general consensus, acceptance and understanding must be reached among the people concerning what traditional values should be preserved and what cross-cultural influences must be borrowed or resisted from other cultures. And this is an ongoing process.

So long as the importance of this consensus is not understood, and so long as attempts to resolve the present dilemma are not made, the generation gap will continue to expand, and confusion, alienation, depression and poor mental health will continue to increase their hold on the Inuit. A continued expansion of negative influences would eventually resolve itself into two separate groups: the very old and traditional

Inuit and the "modern" Inuit who are much influenced by white culture. From there the ultimate resolution would be one entity, that is, the "modern Inuit," the Inuit much influenced by the white.

It is therefore essential that a strong effort be made by both the young and the old to share in the development of a new understanding of themselves as people and to strive together to determine their culture as a people. We are now arriving at a critical point in this cultural transition, both historically and psychologically. The elderly could allow the youth to begin to take responsibility for the future. At the same time, the youth could take positive action. They could share more of their personal concerns with the elderly and begin to accept the advice, concerns and words of the older Inuit.[20] Ultimately, this bridging of the generation gap would result in a unique and culturally rooted approach to helping, with advice bubbling up from within Inuit society.

I am not, of course, proposing that helping skills applied and adopted successfully in southern areas are to be ignored; but maybe they should be. Many of these skills have been given a fair start among the Inuit and at this point can or cannot be used, depending upon their value as evaluated by members of the culture. Research has already determined that some southern methods are useful, such as aspects of Existential Psychology, but others, such as Gestalt therapy, are really quite useless.

Taking Action

Much depends upon the basic strategy of including all age groups of present Inuit society. Several directions are indicated if the development of a culturally relevant approach to helping is to occur.

1. The elderly must become involved in the activities of the youth. They must understand them and exercise patience and tolerance. The elderly must accept that some things will change and accept that responsibility will gradually be shifted towards younger members of the society. The elderly must be prepared to accept advice from more youthful members and to enter into discussions with youth on issues wherein compromise is the only alternative to further rifts.

2. The youth must acknowledge the expertise and knowledge of the elderly and be prepared to share their own personal experiences and to request advice. The youth must also be prepared to provide advice to the elderly and to take and share responsibility for their common future and care. Both requesting and providing advice require some rethinking by contemporary Inuit. Traditionally advice was requested from an *issumatuq* and was then followed. With the cultural changes there have also been changes in the methods of requesting and providing advice. This needs to be explored between the youth and the elders, and appropriate

methods could be developed that are based on tradition and yet take contemporary thinking into account.

3. A culturally specific approach to helping that old and young believe to be of value should be studied and perhaps embodied in a culturally appropriate training program to be taught by and to Inuit. This may be a training program very different from that usually developed by white Westerners. Traditional helping approaches may be included, and some skills and techniques may perhaps be borrowed or be entirely new. What we are looking for here is a synthesis of all Inuit ways that the Inuit will find acceptable and want to share among themselves by teaching one another.

4. In the final analysis, this problem is a cultural and political problem that only the particular culture affected can solve. White influences in the Arctic have resulted in changes in Inuit culture. However, the maintenance of a continuity between traditional culture and the emerging culture is up to the people themselves. Although whites can assist in this process, they can not be the primary developers or carriers of the techniques. The Inuit must actively utilize their psychological skills and provide culturally relevant helping. Though whites could be of assistance in certain academic aspects of a training program, they must relinquish the process of "helping" to the Inuit themselves. The Inuit are the only ones who can take responsibility for making further changes in their own culture.

Summary and Conclusion

Suicide was an aspect of traditional Inuit culture that was held in respect and was arrived at only after personal decision through the process of *ajurnarmat*. In recent times, however, suicides have become symptomatic of a very profound lack of cultural identification, traditional knowledge and intergenerational understanding among young Inuit. To deal with the problems of suicide and cultural collapse, Inuit of all generations must resolve to break through the generation gap and undertake the development of a culturally relevant approach to helping.

Among the traditional approaches we have been identified are the use of *ajurnarmat, issumatuq* and silent acceptance of what cannot be changed. Along with these basic skills are the ability to listen intently and ensure the helper understands what is being stated, and the ability to give advice. The concepts of *ajurnarmat* and *issumatuq* appear to me to be the most applicable today — realizing that problems can be changed and that change is dependent upon the strength and direction of Inuit within their culture. However, silent acceptance may result in continued interference by whites and an application of approaches that may not be acceptable or of assistance to Inuit culture.[21]

The Inuit can be assisted in their endeavour by professionals of various cultural orientations, but it is crucial that the Inuit themselves direct and participate in the process, for only by acting as the agents of their own fate will they be able to recover anything like their traditional psychological resources and strengths.

Summary and Conclusion

The presentation in Chapters 1 to 4 has relied upon a culture-specific design which has provided a systematic and consistent method to investigate Inuit culture and guide the reader through a process of cultural insight. The primary purposes of the design are to invite general inquirers and those in helping professions to approach "helping" from within the framework of a specific culture, and to encourage inquirers to embark upon their own investigations of culture-specific helping within their own and other cultures. Further, the design is intended to determine those methods that may be most effective in the establishment and maintenance of good mental health within a culture. The design is based upon the view that traditional folkways are just as valid within a culture as Western notions are to a member of a Western group, and that no outside group has the right to disregard traditional customs and methods or presuppose that another culture requires new ideologies to be imposed upon it.

At Level I of the design, the level of the physical survival of the group, it becomes clear that in order to physically survive in the Arctic, personal tragedies had to be overcome with little disruption to the camp. Simple physical survival had to take priority over all other camp concerns. The shamans held great power and influence because they assisted the group in maintaining harmony with the spirits. It was the shaman who would ascertain the cause of personal ill-fortune, which could affect the well-being of the entire group. The shaman had the skills to recognize when an individual or individuals had caused displeasure among the spirits, and the shaman also had the skills to appease the spirits and restore security and harmony to the camp. The shaman had the powers to heal the infirm, change or influence nature and enhance the physical well-being of camp members. The shaman was recognized by the group for her or his unique qualities, whether they were of the nature of an infirmity, bodily strength or great intelligence. Combining with the power and skills of the shaman came strict observance of rituals and taboos.

The Inuit held a belief that each individual possessed two souls: a name soul and a human soul. The souls were essential to Inuit philosophy and psychology. Exploration for strengths of character within the name soul was encouraged, and the human soul sought knowledge and skills to survive. The souls combined in spiritual search and struggle. The strength and personality of an individual were gathered from the two souls and influenced by the spirits and the powers of the shaman. The human soul gave the physical strengths and appearance of the individual and was exterior and visible, while the name soul was interior and private.

The Inuit participated in a constant spiritual search. The challenges of life were those of the mind, as well as those of physical endurance, which combined to focus upon survival and enhance the strengths of the souls. During times of struggle because of old age or emotional trauma, suicide was an honourable exit. Through the process of *ajurnarmat* a decision was made that suicide would alleviate the burden. Suicide was honourable because it acknowledged the importance and need to survive of the other camp members. Spiritually, the individual was ready to accept the challenge of death, and the concept of the souls would ensure his or her return when the situation improved.

All these factors at Level I of the design have provided the reader with insight into the highly complex systems and skills that assisted the Inuit culture to maintain good mental health while getting on with the tasks of survival.

Level IIA of the culture-specific design has provided the reader an insight into the group's means of social and psychological survival. The social and psychological survival of the Inuit depended upon two factors: relationships within the group, and modes of helping that were cultur-ally designed and accepted. Relationships within traditional Inuit cul-ture consisted of partnerships and family networks. The partnerships were critical to the physical survival of the group. The emphasis within these partnerships was security and affected the emotional harmony within the group. Extended family networks provided for cooperation, distribution of food, and a fair amount of flexibility despite their apparent cohesion. This security, combined with the security the shaman and concept of the souls provided, enhanced the psychological well-being and emotional harmony of the camp.

Within the extended family network were several nuclear families units, with each member having particular roles and responsibilities.

These roles and responsibilities secured the family well-being and ultimately enhanced the well-being of the camp. Marital bonds provided the roots of the nuclear family. Within these bonds, several characteristics combined to strengthen the initial bonding. The division of labour and mutual interdependence between marriage partners made each a helper to the other in their efforts to survive.

The Inuit employed consistent techniques to reduce anxiety and promote cooperative well-being. These approaches provide insight into the thought patterns of the Inuit, particularly the concepts of: (1) *ajurnarmat*, a method of choosing a course of action in order to relieve stress and emotional frustration, (2) silent acceptance if a matter could not be changed and (3) seeking the advice of an individual possessing *issuma* if a change was considered possible. These three ways combined to establish effective helping skills such as carefully listening, empathy and positive regard, and the ability to give advice and receive respect for the wisdom of that advice. Some of the traditional aspects of helping, such as silent acceptance, respect for the elderly and strong family ties, appear to remain in Inuit culture. The would-be helper needs to understand and utilize these approaches as appropriate helping skills.

The helper must also be aware of extraneous influences upon the culture and how these influences have affected the culture—issues explored at Level IIB of the design. It appears that the earliest extraneous influences upon the Inuit came from whalers around 1590 on Baffin Island. More intense influences began in 1820, again on Baffin Island. The results of these influences included disease and starvation and the death of one-third of the Inuit population by 1900.

Whalers, explorers and traders had other effects upon the Inuit. These influences included the introduction of European materials, such as fire arms, traps and cooking utensils. However, the missionaries had the greatest impact upon traditional helping approaches, and this is most evident in their attempts to disqualify the power of the shaman and the spirits. The missionaries moved in without invitation to Inuit camps, and lived and worked with the people, learning their language and customs. The missionaries developed a trust with the Inuit and, partly through their knowledge of pharmacopoeia and their use of European medicines, they gained respect from the Inuit. Having gained this respect, they began to influence the Inuit with European religions and beliefs. One of the missionaries' first tasks was to discredit the shaman and effectively to take the power the shaman had previously been honoured with. This seizure of power interrupted a traditional approach to helping. The shaman had brought to the camp a security and peace of mind that assisted the camp to put its energies into the hunt and into getting on with survival. Throughout the Arctic, the shaman's power to help was diminished by the extraneous influences and this also effectively limited the security of the hunt. With this help gone, the camps moved closer to the trading posts, disrupting the traditional living arrangements of the Inuit.

The detailed accounts of Pelly Bay and Sanikiluaq provide insight into the power and influence of the missionaries and their religions. By comparing the two groups, it becomes clearer that physical survival and psychological and social survival strengths determine the ability of a group to withstand external influences and to take from these influences only those skills that will benefit the group. Strength at these two levels allows a slower, more gradual and thought-out process of cultural transition. The Pelly Bay group in particular continues to use the helping approaches of *ajurnarmat*, silent acceptance and *issumatuq*, and the skills of intent listening, queries to insure that the listener has heard and understood the speaker, and respectful advice giving and receiving. The continued use of these skills has an effect upon helping among the Inuit today. At Level III of the design, the experience of the individual in the group, these traditional techniques are critical to emotional and psychological well-being.

Traditionally, spiritual goals sustained a world view and guided daily activities, which significantly encouraged good mental health among the Inuit. With the disruption of traditional patterns of physical, psychological and social survival, a void appears to have been created which affects personal development and one's sense of meaning in life. Inuit youth have been affected most directly. The result is an existential vacuum, boredom, alcoholism, violence and suicide. The white society has imposed upon the Inuit white technologies and goals that may make little sense to the Inuit youth, and much less to the Inuit elder. The traditional will to explore, set new goals and struggle to attain inner contentment and harmonious communal life is lost among many Inuit youth, and appropriate substitutes are not there.

Some youth have believed suicide to be an acceptable escape from the vacuum in which they have found themselves. And alcohol, loss of love ones and climatic conditions seem to be contributing factors. Each summer as these youth travelled on the land with their parents and elders, they were allowed a glimpse into the past, into what was and what could have been. When this experience was blocked by weather conditions, and other factors came into play, suicides increased. Suicide may have been seen as an effort to return to a traditionally accepted and respected response to a difficult situation.

The response of each Inuk to the turmoil caused within and without them by the white intrusion appears to be tied to their traditional understandings and lifestyles, or lack thereof. It would thus only make sense that helping among the Inuit would take into account these traditions. Approaches to helping among the Inuit, of necessity, need to include *ajurnarmat, issumatuq,* and silent acceptance of what can not be changed, listening and making sure one understands what is being said.

Traditionally, few questions were asked; rather, through deep reflection upon words and thoughts, the listener understood all that was being expressed and how the speaker viewed her or his world. The critical skill of advice giving is also necessary—the ability to give advice and be respected for that ability. Some of the basic requirements are respect, trust and responsibility to follow through on action, thus taking the advice offered. Unlike in times past, no longer can a group member be encouraged to take advice or risk the consequences of banishment. Now it is necessary for youth to respect the advice given and trust the person providing the advice. This is not to imply that respect, trust and personal responsibility were not present traditionally, but today they have become more necessary and obvious. Another traditional way to follow is to use group self-determination to work through the generational gap among the Inuit. The Inuit must direct and participate in this process, because only by acting as agents of their own fate will they be able to express their traditional strengths.

The hardships of physical survival in the Arctic have historically demanded cooperation, sharing and trust. The psychological and social survival systems of the Inuit were clearly a result of what was needed to survive physically, and they traditionally incorporated all of these factors into a healthy environment for group, family and individual. Even today, because of the climate and its demands, in order to live in the Arctic, one must have awareness of and an ability to use some of the traditional notions of Inuit culture. If not, one could easily die in this harsh environment or go mad. Visitors to the Arctic are forced, out of good common sense, to accept, adapt and utilize traditional ways.

The reader is reminded that this entire presentation has provided but a glimpse into Inuit culture. The particular groups that provided information for this text reside in the Kitikmeot (Arctic coast) and Baffin regions of Canada's Northwest Territories. Caution should be used in transferring this material to other Inuit groups, and particular caution is encouraged with respect to Greenlandic and Alaskan groups. But readers are heartily encouraged to use the culture-specific design to learn of other cultures or investigate their own. The design offers a guide into the intricacies and complexities of culture.

The Canadian Inuit possessed an effective traditional psychology and sociology. We have glimpsed some of these characteristics of Inuit culture and its traditional helping approaches and skills. It now becomes apparent how very accepting and tolerant the Inuit are, while residing in a complicated and exacting culture. Southern white attitudes and superiority complexes must indeed take a second place to the profound traditional skills and approaches used by the Inuit to survive physically, psychologically and socially. Inuit standards of cooperation, perseverance and initiative far outweigh the materialism and individualism encouraged by southern educational and social systems. Respect and trust remain the essential underpinnings of helping approaches and skills among the Inuit.

The Inuit of the Canadian Arctic are a strong culture. As the intrusion of southern groups continues, immense cultural changes are likely to occur, and indeed some critical folkways are certain to be lost while others will change. The results for the Inuit can only be viewed over time. A terrible barrage of new concepts has been imposed upon Arctic residents in a relatively short time span. Retention of respect for the elderly and strong family ties will be valuable assets in the struggles of the Inuit. However, the most critical understanding is that the Inuit must take control of their own destiny. An essential component of this destiny is the area of social services and particularly helping practices. This area includes training, implementation of programs and financial responsibility for these programs.

It is the Inuit who will continue to reside in the Arctic. Cultural visitors cannot continue to determine the needs of the Inuit or take control of services, and southerners must respect this. As I have demonstrated, the Inuit have traditional skills and approaches that have resulted in healthy emotional well-being. The present Northwest Territorial Legislative Assembly and Executive Council include a majority of First Nations Peoples and, with negotiations regarding land claims, the Inuit are in a position to take control. Though cultural transitions have been difficult, the Inuit are a strong culture, one that has suffered severe trauma over centuries and survived. This culture continues to survive and to seek a balance with nature, while retaining traditional values. Today, the Inuit recognize the importance of a working knowledge of the dominant white, southern cultures, and they will draw out, encourage and use the best of both worlds for their children and generations to come.

Appendix 1:
A Summary of the Design for Culture-Specific Helping

A culturally specific approach begins with an exploration of the traditional helping systems within a group. Of necessity, such an exploration is accomplished with the aid of anthropological information. The effectiveness of traditional approaches is not to be underestimated, any more than one can ignore the strength of traditional ties in helping patterns. Social work and helping will have to be developed or adapted with approaches peculiar to both the history and current needs of the culture for which the helping is intended. This reflects the basic premise of "culture-specific social work" and "culture-specific helping."

This design was developed for use in culture-specific social work with a major emphasis upon helping. To ensure that the design of any program is rooted in the culture and appropriate to it, as well as politically and administratively viable, three steps are necessary. The first step is to ensure the participation of knowledgeable, articulate and influential members of the culture. The second is to explore, identify and understand the philosophy, psychology and traditional patterns of interpersonal interaction that prevail within the group. And the third step is to embark upon a program of helping that involves support and facilitation, and to build evaluative criteria into the design to gauge the effectiveness of efforts to provide appropriate culture-specific helping.

These steps do not take up the questions of leadership roles or the political context. Rather, I emphasize the need for a new approach. With respect to leadership, Western helpers must take a back seat and give respect to the members of the client culture, who must, in turn, be certain that it is up to them to seize the power to initiate the process. What counts here is that the responsibility is two-fold, something like a transaction, in which concern for others is exchanged for an understanding of each other and what is appropriate in the helping context. If non-members are to be included in the process of helping, their roles should be as supportive facilitators. The members of the particular culture should become the initiators, leaders, designers and ultimately those who will take responsibility for ongoing re-evaluation and initiation of change. Clearly the control and power must come from within the culture. Cultural differences need to be acknowledged and respected.

Levels of the Design

How does one investigate the world view of another when one is a member of another culture? To shed light upon this, I have developed a phased approach. This approach begins with physical survival, and the assumption that physical survival is the basic means of entry into the world view of another culture. This notion makes it possible for us to understand the systems and patterns of interaction that take place within a group. Thus, using appropriate anthropological methods and approaches, Level I is explored and through this exploration some traditional factors that have been essential to the physical survival of the group are identified.

Following this exploration, Level IIA is explored. This level lends insight into factors critical to the social and psychological survival of the group. It is essential that the student of culture strives to understand the cultural system from the vantage point of the world view of the group under study.

Level IIB is then explored and one notes the external factors that have influenced the culture.

At Level III, the student has the opportunity to make sense of the individual within the group and sees what is gained when the individual is identified as a valued member and what is lost when he or she ceases to be valued. Once the inquirer reaches Level III, patterns of behaviour, thought and traditional helping techniques will emerge and be made sense of as a group function. In order to demonstrate these necessary ways of helping, such as empathy, understanding and respect, the methods and approaches must be specific to the context and must be based upon culturally appropriate factors and upon effective communication within that context.

The sequence of the design begins with environmental factors, moves into psychological and sociological factors, and then moves to the individual. At that point, a sense of reality, clarity and consistency may be achieved. The drawbacks of the design serve as its check points. First, the investigation cannot be carried out without the full cooperation of group members. Second, attempts to apply the design will fail if one attempts to impose foreign world views and values upon the group members with whom one is working. Third, the helping process itself is lengthy and complicated, as is the process of cultural experience, and so neither can be achieved in a short time. And finally, the evaluative process must reflect the values and notions of the culture under study. Thus, in every specific cultural investigation the method of evaluation will be equally specific.

Appendix 2:
Translations of
Key Terms from Inuktitut

communication competence
ᑐᑭᓯᑎᑦᓯᖅᑭᓂᖅ
tukisititsiqqiniq

interpersonal relationships
ᐃᓅᖃᑎᒌᓂᖅ
inuuqatigiiniq

consanguineal bonds
ᐃᓚᒌᓂᖅ ᐊᖏᔪᖅᑲᑎᒍᑦ
ilagiiniq angijuqqaatigut

affinal bonds
ᐃᓚᒌᓂᖅ ᐊᐃᐸᕐᒥᒍᑦ
ilagiiniq aiparmigut

collaborative relationships
ᓴᓇᖃᑎᒌᓐᓂᖅ
sanaqatigiinniq

group communalism
ᐱᖁᑎᖃᖃᑎᒌᓐᓂᖅ
piqutiqaqatigiinniq

Notes

1.   The term *Inuit* is synonymous with "Eskimo." The language of the Canadian Inuit is Inuktitut. Inuit means "the people" and is the term used by the Inuit to describe themselves. The singular is *Inuk*, the dual is *Inuuk* and the plural is *Inuit*. The term is nonsexist and thus used for both males and females.

2.   "Traditional Inuit" refers to the time prior to settlement in permanent communities.

3.   In defining and describing the climatic conditions and the struggle for survival of the traditional Inuit, one must realize that the Inuit were well adapted to this lifestyle. They were inventive and developed many techniques to facilitate survival. The struggles of the Inuit, as viewed by the Europeans, were indeed harsh, for the Europeans had not adapted to the conditions. But for the Inuit, it was a way of life to be accepted, one which provided challenge. I do not wish to imply that the struggle of life was harsh beyond human endurance, for if such had been the case, the culture would not have succeeded. Rather, the struggle forced certain adaptations on the people which they had to accept both physically and emotionally. The environment provided the context within which the cultural responses can be viewed as both creative and ingenious.

4.   *Qallunaaq* is an Inuktitut term referring to anyone or anything non-Inuit. In various dialects the spelling and pronunciation may differ, but the meaning remains the same, i.e., *kabluna, qablunaa,* etc. For simplicity, this term will be used to indicate persons of non-

Inuit origin residing with and/or influencing the Canadian Inuit. The "steady involvement" of the *qallunaaq* refers specifically to the period following the visible organization of government structures in the Arctic, i.e., the permanent establishment of government buildings and personnel, medical centres, school and administrative facilities.

5.   "Just to Survive," a poem written by the author. Many Inuit have read the poem and describe it as portraying a sense of the Inuit's deep feelings towards and with nature.

6.   I have had the good fortune to be entrusted with knowledge of the traditional practice of shamanism by some elderly Inuit who previously practiced, and in some cases continue to practice, the art. For the sake of that trust, I will portray the art of shamanism only in a general way, providing specific examples only when necessary, and in all cases omitting personal identifying information. Perhaps some scholars may be critical of my resolve to withhold more specific information and may allege a certain inability on my part to divorce emotion from the investigative accumulation of facts. Be that as it may, were I capable of such divorce I would neither consider myself a student of culture nor have been allowed to remain among the Inuit for so long. Thus I write such information as I have gathered in an effort to share what I have learned and yet respect the confidentiality my informants requested of me. The general content of these discussions has been paraphrased and is presented within the context of their effects upon helping among the Inuit.

7.   *Turnqaniq* in Inuktitut refers to "soul." Various dialects utilize various words; however, the concept remains the same. The term has also been translated as "spirit" or "his or her own spirit or spirits." As with all nouns in Inuktitut, the change from singular to dual and plural involves merely a change in the ending. For the purposes of clarity, the singular third person nominative possessive form will be used. Thus, *turnqaniq* will be used for both singular and plural. A *turnqaniq* is to be distinguished from a supernatural spirit.

8.   Netsilik group. This group is located in the Gjøa Haven to Pelly Bay area.

9. *Ajurnarmat*: an Inuktitut term meaning "it can't be changed." The root word is *ajurna*. The term has various spellings in different dialects, e.g., *ayorama, aijugnaq, ayugnaq*, etc. The crucial element of this concept concerns the thought process necessary to determine whether or not a matter can be changed. See Briggs (1970, 364) for a good discussion of *ayugnaq*.

10. I would note that in the present cultural transition state, communal efforts and attitudes are rapidly deteriorating and that there is in the Arctic immense variation in intensity of cooperative efforts from one group to another. However, the scope of this chapter is upon early patterns as defined previously.

11. *Issuma* is the root word for thought, or ability to think clearly. *Issumatuq* is an Inuktitut term indicating the possession of wisdom. For the purposes of this book, the latter concept will be designated by the third person, present tense form, and the only variant will be that of the root word itself. The term *issuma* has various spellings in different dialects, e.g., *ihuma*, but the meaning remains the same. See Briggs (1970) for a good discussion of *ihuma*.

12. An answer would indicate that the resource helper has a suggestion, silence indicates that the helper is considering the matter, and *amai* means the helper has considered the matter and does not know a course of action.

13. See also Sissions (1973). This information was gathered from Sissions and from personal conversations with Shooyook, Aiyaoot, Napachee-Kadluk, and Ernie Lyall of Spence Bay.

14. Arvilinghuarmiut is the area now known as Pelly Bay, Northwest Territories.

15. The quotations indicate exact statements made by informants, as translated by an interpreter.

16. Wallace (1970, 188-99) provides an excellent discussion of revitalization. As defined by Wallace, the activities on the Belcher Islands clearly were a revitalization.

17. The references cited were used to support the incidents, which were personally related to me by several of the participants.

18.   *Inummariit* is translated from Inuktitut as "the free Inuk," one who
       has struggled and overcome physical, emotional and spiritual
       barriers. Brody (1975, 125-45) provides an excellent discussion of
       this term.

19.   It must be noted that various agencies in the North have made
       sincere attempts to provide an alternative and useful counselling
       service for the Inuit. However, only recently have these ap-
       proaches become culturally relevant. Previously, the services were
       conducted according to basically southern styles.

20.   This book speaks generally of Canadian Inuit across the Arctic, but
       the reader should note that each family unit differs in its internal
       relationships. The author emphasizes the growing numbers of
       alienated youth and elderly in Inuit society but by no means wishes
       to imply that these constitute the majority of Inuit.

21.   The culturally relevant approaches I have presented in this chapter
       have been discussed at length with Inuit of all ages, both in groups
       and individually. The recommendations provided represent a
       summary of those discussions. It is not my intention to "prescribe"
       to a culture other than my own; rather, I acted as a facilitator and
       recordkeeper during the conversations. Though the errors in the
       reporting of the comments and recommendations are my respon-
       sibility, the thought, strength and realism of this section results
       from the careful thoughts of many Inuit concerned for their future
       and that of their children.

Bibliography

Allport, G.W. (1978). *Becoming.* New Haven: Yale University Press.

Alvarez, A. (1972). *The Savage God.* New York: Random House.

Asuni, T. (1975). "Existing concepts of mental illness in different forms of treatment." In *Mental Health Services in Developing Countries,* edited by T. Baasher et al. Geneva, Switzerland: World Health Organization.

Ayaruaq, J. (1968). *John Ayaruaq Unipkarnga Inushimi.* Autobiography. Ottawa: Department of Indian Affairs and Northern Development.

Baasher, T., G. Carstairs, R. Giel and F. Hassler (1975). *Mental Health Services in Developing Countries.* Geneva, Switzerland: World Health Organization.

Back, G. (1836). *Narrative of the Arctic Land Expedition to the Mouth of the Great Fish River.* London: J. Murray.

Balikci, A. (1970). *The Netsilik Eskimo.* Garden City, N.Y.: Museum of Natural History.

Benedict, R. (1934). *Patterns of Culture.* Boston: Houghton-Mifflin.

Boas, F. (1888). *The Central Eskimo.* Sixth annual report of the Bureau of Ethnology. Washington D.C.: Smithsonian Institute.

Brice-Bennett, C. (1976). "Inuit Land Use in the East Central Canadian Arctic." In *Inuit Land and Occupancy Project,* Vol. 1, edited by M. Freeman. Ottawa: Department of Indian and Northern Affairs.

Briggs, J. (1970). *Never in Anger.* Cambridge, Mass.: Harvard University Press.

Briggs, J. (1974). "Eskimo Women, Makers of Men." In *Many Sisters, Women in Cross-Cultural Perspective,* edited by C.J. Matthiason New York: Free Press.

Brody, H. (1975). *The People's Land.* Markham, Ont.: Penguin.

Brody, H. (1976). "Inummariit: The Real Eskimo." *Inuit Land and Occupancy Project,* Vol. II, edited by M. Freeman. Ottawa: Department of Indian and Northern Affairs.

Brody, H. (1977). "Alcohol: Change and the Industrial Frontier." *Etudes Inuit Studies* 1(12): 31-47.

Bruemmer, F. (1971). "Whalers of the North." *The Beaver* (winter): 44-55.

Canada (1918-80). *Vital Statistics.* Ottawa: Department of Health.

Coccola, R.D., and P. King (1955). *Ayorama.* Toronto: Oxford University Press.

Crowe, K.J. (1974). *A History of the Original Peoples of Northern Canada.* Montreal: Queen's University Press.

Delany, L. (1972). "The Other Bodies in the River." In *Black Psychology,* edited by R.L. Jones. New York: Harper and Row.

Durkheim, E. (1951). *Suicide.* Glencoe, Ill.: Free Press.

Fanon, F. (1968). *The Wretched of the Earth.* New York: Grove Press.

Frankl, V. (1967). *Psychotherapy and Existentialism.* New York: Washington Square Press.

Frankl, V. (1970) *Man's Search for Meaning.* New York: Washington Square Press.

Freeman, M., ed. (1976). *Inuit Land Use and Occupancy Project.* Vol. II. Ottawa: Department of Indian and Northern Affairs.

Freuchen, P. (1961). *Book of the Eskimo.* New York: Bramhall House.

Gilligan, C. (1982). *In a Different Voice.* Cambridge, Mass.: Harvard University Press.

Gilligan, C., et al., eds. (1989). *Mapping the Moral Domain.* Cambridge, Mass.: Harvard University Press.

Guemple, L. (1976). "The Institutional Flexibility of Inuit Social Life." In *Inuit Land and Occupancy Project,* Vol. II, edited by M. Freeman. Ottawa: Department of Indian and Northern Affairs.

Hawkes, E.W. (1916). *The Labrador Eskimo.* Memo 91 of the Geographical Survey of Canada. Ottawa: Department of Northern Affairs.

Health and Welfare Canada (1919-80). Statistical reports. Ottawa: Department of Statistics.

Hebert, W. (1976). *Eskimo.* Toronto: Collins.

Hewett, M. (1970). *Mackenzie Zone Information Book.* Yellowknife: Health and Welfare Canada.

Innukshuk, R., and S. Cowan (1976). *We Don't Live in Snow Houses Now.* Ottawa: Canadian Arctic Producers Limited.

Ivey, A., and N. Gluckstern (1976). *Basic Influencing Skills: Participants Manual.* North Amherst, Mass.: Microtraining.

Ivey, A. (1977). *Basic Attending Skills.* North Amherst, Mass.: Microtraining.

Ivey, A. (1980). *Counseling and Psychotherapy: Connections and Applications.* New York: Prentice-Hall.

Ivey, A., with L. Simek-Downing (1980). *Counseling and Psychotherapy: Skills, Theory, and Practice.* Englewood Cliffs, N.J.: Prentice-Hall.

Ivey, A. (1981). "Counseling and Psychotherapy: Toward a New Perspective." In *Cross-Cultural Counseling and Psychotherapy,* edited by A. Marsella and P. Pedersen. New York: Pergamon Press.

Jackson, G. (1976). "The African Genesis of the Black Perspective in Helping." *Professional Psychology* (August).

Jackson, G. (1980). "The Emergence of the Black Perspective in Counseling." In *Black Psychology,* edited by R. Jones. New York: Harper and Row.

Jenness, D. (1928). *The People of the Twilight.* New York: Macmillan.

Jones, R., ed. (1980). *Black Psychology.* New York: Harper and Row.

Kalluak, M., ed. (1974). *How Kabloonat Became and Other Inuit Legends.* Yellowknife: Department of Education.

Kappi, L. (1977). *Inuit Legends.* Yellowknife: Department of Education.

Kitano, H., and S. Stanley (1972). "The Model Minorities." *Journal of Social Issues* 29(2): 1-9.

Klagsburn, F. (1977). *Youth and Suicide.* New York: Pocket Books.

Lafromboise, T.D. (1988). "American Indian Mental Health Policy." *American Psychologist* 43(5): 388-97.

Issumatuq

Lantis, M. (1959). "Folk Medicine and Hygiene: Lower Kuskokwion and Nunivak–Nelson Island Areas." *Anthropological Papers* (University of Alaska) 8(1): 1-76.

Laughlin, W.S. (1976). "Hunting: An Integrating Biobehaviour System." *Inuit Land and Occupancy Project*, Vol. II, edited by M. Freeman. Ottawa: Department of Indian and Northern Affairs.

Marsella, A. (1979). "Applications of Traditional Asian Medicine to Contemporary Psychiatric Services in Developing Nations." Paper presented at the Fifth Annual International Conference on Traditional Asian Medicine, Canberra, Australia, September 1979.

Maslow, A. (1968). *Toward a Psychology of Being*. New York: Nostrand.

Maslow, A. (1976). *The Farthest Reaches of Human Nature*. New York: Penguin.

May, R. (1969). "Existential Psychotherapy: Six Talks for CBC Radio." Toronto: CBC Publications.

Mead, M., ed. (1955). *Cultural Patterns and Technological Change*. New York: Montol.

Mead, M. (1978). *Culture and Commitment*. Garden City, N.J.: Anchor Press/ Doubleday.

Millard, A.E. (1930). *Southern Baffin Island*. Ottawa: Department of the Interior.

Minor, K.M. (1973-83). Field notes.

Minor, K.M. (1979). "Helping: A Traditional Inuit Approach." Unpublished.

Minor, K.M. (1980a). "Customers and Converts." Unpublished.

Minor, K.M. (1980b). "Suicide: Past and Present." Unpublished.

Minor, K.M., and F.J. Turner (1986). "Special Status Groups." *Canadian Social Welfare*, 2nd edition, edited by J.C. Turner and F.J. Turner. Don Mills, Ont.: Collier Macmillan.

Minor, K.M. (in progress). "Collected Poems and Short Stories of Ten Years in the Arctic."

Missionary Oblates of Mary Immaculate (1920-45). *Link*. Churchill, Manitoba.

Moore, B.M. (1974). "Cultural Differences and Counseling Perspective." *Texas Personnel and Guidance Journal* 3: 39-44.

Nelson, C., L. Kelley and D. McPherson (1985). "Recovering Support in Social Work Practice." *Canadian Social Work Review*.

Nelson, R.K. (1976). "The Inuk as Hunter." In *Inuit Land and Occupancy Project*, Vol. II, edited by M. Freeman. Ottawa: Department of Indian and Northern Affairs.

Nobels, W. (1972). "African Philosophy: Foundations for Black Psychology." *Black Psychology*, edited by R. Jones. New York: Harper and Row.

Nobels, W. (1974). "Africanity: Its Role in Black Families." *The Black Scholar* (June 10-17).

Northwest Territories (1965-80). *Sanikiluaq, N.W.T.* Administrative field reports. Yellowknife.

Nuligak (1966). *I, Nuligak.* Translated and edited by M. Metayer. New York: Simon and Schuster.

Nwachuku, U., and A. Ivey (1989). *Teaching Culture-Specific Counseling Using Microtraining Technology.* Amherst, Mass. Unpublished.

Oblate Fathers of the Hudson's Bay Vicariate (1943-91). *Eskimo: Country, Customs, Catholic Missionaries.* Churchill, Manitoba.

O'Neil, J. (1979). "Health Care in an Inuit Settlement: A Study of Conflict and Congruence in Inuit Adaptation to the Cosmopolitan Medical System." Master's thesis, University of Saskatchewan.

Pedersen, P. (1976). "The Field of Intercultural Counseling." In *Counseling Across Cultures,* edited by P. Pederson et al. Honolulu: University Press of Hawaii.

Pedersen, P. (1977). "The Triad Model of Cross-Cultural Counselor Training." *Personnel and Guidance Journal* 2: 94-100.

Price, R. (1970). *The Howling Arctic.* Toronto: Peter Martin.

Rasky, F. (1976). *The Polar Voyagers.* Toronto: McGraw-Hill Ryerson.

Rasmussen, K. (1931). "The Netsilik Eskimo: Social Life and Spiritual Culture." *Report of the Fifth Thule Expedition 1921-24,* 8 (1-2). Copenhagen.

Rogers, C. (1942). *Counseling and Psychotherapy.* Cambridge, Mass.: Houghton-Mifflin.

Rogers, C. (1957). "The Necessary and Sufficient Conditions of Therapeutic Personality Change." *Journal of Consulting Psychology* 21: 95-103.

Rogers, C. (1970). *On Encounter Groups.* New York: Harper and Row.

Royal Canadian Mounted Police (RCMP) (1921, 1941). Reports. Ottawa: King's Printer.

Royal North-West Mounted Police (RNWMP) (1916, 1917-18, 1919.) Reports. Ottawa: King's Printer.

Ruben, B.D. (1977). "Guidelines for Cross Cultural Communication Effectiveness." *Group and Organization Studies* 2 (4): 470-79.

Shweder, R.A., and E.J. Bourne (1984). "Does the concept of person vary cross-culturally?" In *Culture Theory: Essays on Mind, Self, and Emotion*, edited by R.A. Scweder and R.A. Levine. New York: Cambridge University Press.

Sissions, J. (1973). *Judge of the Far North*. Toronto: McClelland and Stewart.

Stairs, A. (1988). "Beyond cultural inclusion: An Inuit example of indigenous educational development." In *Minority Education: From Shame to Struggle*, edited by J. Cummins and T. Skutnabb-Kangas. Clevedon, Avon, England: Multilingual Matters.

Stairs, A. (in press). "Learning processes and teaching roles in native education: Cultural base and cultural brokerage." In *Aboriginal Languages and Education*, edited by K. McLeod, S. Morris and M. Danesi.

Stefanson, V. (1921). *The Friendly Arctic*. New York: Macmillan.

Stefanson, V. (1951). *My Life with the Eskimo*. New York: Macmillan.

Sue, S. (1977). "Psychological Theory and Implications for Asian Americans." *Personnel and Guidance Journal* 55(7): 381-89.

Van de Velde, F. (1956). "Les negles du patage des phoques pris par la chasse aux aglus." *Anthropologica* 3: 5-14.

Wallace, A.F. (1970). *Culture and Personality*. 2nd ed. New York: Random House.

Wenzel, G.W., and A. Stairs, (in press). "I am I and the environment: Inuit hunting, community, and identity." *Journal of Medical Anthropology*.

Whitney, H. (1910). *Hunting with the Eskimos*. New York: Century Company.

Also from Fernwood Publishing

Feminist Pedagogy
An Autobiographical Approach
Anne-Louise Brookes

Beyond the Limits of the Law
Corporate Crime and Law and Order
John McMullan

Re-Thinking the Administration of Justice
Dawn Currie and Brian MacLean eds.

State Theories
From Liberalism to the Challenge of Feminism
(second edition)
Murray Knuttila

Deconstructing a Nation
Immigration, Multiculturalism and Racism in 90s Canada
Vic Satzewich ed.

The Crisis of Socialist Theory
Strategy and Practice
Joe Roberts ed.

and the Basics from Fernwood...

Issumatuq
Learning from the Traditonal Healing Wisdom
of the Canadian Inuit
Kit Minor

Man's Will to Hurt
Investigating the Causes, Supports
and Varieties of His Violence
Joseph A. Kuypers

Elusive Justice
Beyond the Marshall Inquiry
Joy Mannette ed.